Praise

'Jose Ucar's insightful book is for anyone navigating the complex world of international business. With a focus on authenticity and simplicity, it provides practical strategies to foster genuine connections, enhance communication and, ultimately, boost productivity and results.'
> — **Cecilia Taieb**, Global Director of Communications, SEAT and CUPRA, www.cupraofficial.com

'*Global Influence* encourages the reader to use different emotional and internally led frameworks, to navigate the global business world. The Global Influence Model explores our differences while focusing on solutions for business leaders to amplify their international impact. If you are serious about expanding your influence and adapting in situations to get the most from your audience, this is the book for you.'
> — **Nicola Towse**, Senior Market, Strategy and Planning Manager, Procter & Gamble UK & Ireland, www.pg.co.uk

'This insightful and thought-provoking book delves into the strategies and techniques that business leaders can employ to navigate the complexities of the global business landscape. With its clear and concise approach, readers will gain a deeper

understanding of international business dynamics and learn how to effectively solve complex challenges. Prepare to unlock your full potential and make a lasting impact on the global stage with this exceptional read.'
— **Jose Aristimuño**, former Obama official and CEO, VIP Media, www.vipmediasolutions.com

'If you want to have an impact at a global level, you must be able to simplify your message, be adaptable in the way you deliver it and have the ability to connect with audiences from diverse backgrounds. This book will show you how to do this and, when applied, will transform you into a leader with global influence.'
— **Simon Alexander Ong**, international keynote speaker and bestselling author of *Energize*, www.simonalexanderong.com

'Jose Ucar draws on his international experience as well as his skills in communicating for positive impact and influence to bring a unique and practical set of tools to international business leaders. An essential set of tools for today's world.'
— **Brigid Farrell**, intercultural communication specialist and director, AllTalk Training, www.alltalktraining.com

'A must-read book on mastering effective global communication from the charismatic storyteller that

is Jose Ucar. A book I'll be recommending to business leaders and entrepreneurs.'
— **Alex Chisnall**, founder of Podpreneur, and host of the *Screw It, Just Do It* podcast, https://podpreneur.co.uk

'*Global Influence* by Jose Ucar is an exploration of international communication and influence through a different lens. Jose's unique perspective and expertise, together with his stories and practical examples, provide valuable tools and resources to leaders and business owners operating in international environments. I highly recommend this book to gain a deeper understanding of how communication shapes your world and how positive influence can change the way you lead your people to achieve greater results. Don't miss the opportunity to expand your knowledge and perspective by delving into *Global Influence*.'
— **Elliot Kay**, award-winning entrepreneur and expert speaker helping established entrepreneurs become leaders and influencers in their sector, https://elliotkay.com

'If anyone is looking for a dry, theoretical tome on communication – avoid this book! Because Jose's book is fully committed to real-life application of the *how* of becoming a global thinker, influencer and, ultimately, player – whatever your preferred game is. My biggest take-away is to be less vanilla (though it remains my favourite ice cream flavour) and work on

my CQ. This is a great read that speaks to the heart as well as to the mind.'
— **Reza Ram**, management consultant, EY,
Latin dancer and global mind, www.ey.com

'In today's global economy, we must bridge the gap of fear and cultural differences to communicate authentically. This book reveals how leaders can simplify, improve and amplify their international impact, fostering genuine human connections across nations. Embrace authenticity, sharpen communication skills, and lead with confidence to positively influence others and drive remarkable business results.'
— **Neil Cameron**, founder and director,
Cameron Investment Group and
SportWorks, https://sportworksltd.co.uk

'An insightful blend of psychology, communication, and cultural awareness, *Global Influence* is a unique guide for leaders trying to navigate the complexities of our interconnected world. The book challenges fear-based norms and promotes authenticity, providing leaders with the essential tools to enhance their international impact. It breaks new ground in leadership communication, offering a strategic roadmap for building authentic, effective relationships across nations. In an era when AI is a threat to authenticity in business and life, *Global Influence* is a must-read for leaders striving to stand out in the global marketplace.'
— **Cinzia De Santis**, chair and founder, Healing Venezuela, www.healingvenezuela.org

'The ability to communicate and lead with impact is what separates the so-so leaders from the big hitters. This book not only builds you from the foundations – understanding what global influence is – it supports you to develop your own global influence and, not only that, but to exercise it too. This is where the true magic happens. Jose is perfectly placed to lead you on this journey. I'm excited for you to amplify your influence globally!'

— **Liz Hamlet**, internationally known author, strategist, coach and speaker; founder, Spark Succeed and The Antisocial Social Club, www.sparksucceed.co.uk

'In *Global Influence*, business leaders will have the opportunity to explore the essential elements of authentic communication, cultural fluency and transformative leadership. By honing these skills, they will be empowered to achieve unprecedented levels of international success, making a positive impact on a global scale. I highly recommend this book.'

— **Ricardo Schmidt Diaz**, General Manager of Travel Retail APAC, L'Oréal, www.loreal.com

'If you are looking to unlock your *Global Influence*, this book is for you. Learn to bridge cultures, connect minds and inspire success.'

— **Sabrina Stocker**, entrepreneur and investor, www.twocommapr.com

JOSE UCAR

GLOBAL INFLUENCE

Simplify, improve and amplify your
international leadership impact

FOREWORD BY MARIA FRANZONI

R^ethink

First published in Great Britain in 2023
by Rethink Press (www.rethinkpress.com)

© Copyright Jose Ucar

Cover image licensed by Ingram Image

This book is dedicated to my unforgettable and always present grandparents; my supportive, patient and ever-loving papa y mama; my beloved wife; my brother, German; my friend and mentor, Alan Pearce; and all the people who have positively impacted my life.

I also want to dedicate this book to all the international leaders out there who want to improve their ability to influence and create positive change in their expanding businesses and organisations.

Contents

Foreword

What makes a leader influential on a global scale? What does it mean to communicate effectively across borders, cultures, languages and accents, and how do you master this complex art? If you are asking yourself these questions, then this book is for you.

As a mentor to speakers and professionals across the globe, I have worked with influential figures including Neil Armstrong, Anita Roddick and Nassim Nicholas Taleb, and have held senior positions in prominent bureaus such as CSA Celebrity Speakers and London Speaker Bureau, as well as running my own international speakers bureau. I have helped many professionals transform their speaking careers, and Jose Ucar is one of them.

When I met Jose, he immediately resonated with me: his is not just a success story, but a story that demonstrates resilience, adaptability and a deep understanding of global communication – which he shares with us in this book. Jose and I met virtually, but even at this remove I was immediately struck by his big personality, his humour and great passion for bridging communication gaps in international business environments. His sincerity in wanting to help others left a real impression on me. Our collaboration marked the beginning of a transformative journey for Jose – a journey that has culminated in this thought-provoking and insightful book.

Global Influence is a practical handbook for leaders as well as a mirror that reflects the reality of global communication in the business world. Jose explains, with great clarity, the key obstacles that leaders face in trying to communicate effectively across international borders. He identifies fear as a primary factor, but also our desire to fit in, which can compromise our authenticity and make our communication less effective.

As you go deeper into the book, you'll discover effective strategies and helpful concepts to deal with these challenges. Jose outlines how to be authentic in our interactions, how to harness the power of simplicity in communication and how to navigate the nuances of cultural difference. Beyond that, he provides a roadmap for becoming a more effective leader who can inspire, motivate and positively influence others across nations.

Jose's wide-ranging experience of working with global businesses is the basis of the wisdom and practical knowledge he shares in this book. Through his engaging storytelling and pragmatic advice, Jose offers a fresh perspective on the complex area of international business communication.

This book is an invaluable resource, whether you're an established leader or an ambitious professional. You too can master the art of global influence – let Jose show you how.

Maria Franzoni
Former International Speaker Bureau owner
Founder of Speaking Business Academy

Introduction

Businesses keep growing and the world seems to be getting smaller, thanks to technological advancements in communication. Yet the fundamental ability of humans to communicate to connect and impact each other hasn't evolved much. The channels and content may have changed, but we still don't manage to get our message across as effectively as we could, which has a variety of repercussions in life and in business. But why is this?

Let's go back, for a second, to the moment of our birth. A time at which, by nature, we are all genuine. Our origin is undisputed. We are authentic. Then, along the way, life experiences, culture and people begin to sculpt the person we will become, a social individual conditioned to follow rules and standards, to meet expectations and to fit in, causing us to adopt an external authenticity that is almost imposed upon us.

This is where it gets interesting. From this place of adopted authenticity, we go and 'communicate' with one another – and what happens? We pretend to be someone else. We don't display our true self, our true feelings and thoughts, leaving things unsaid, making assumptions, fearing being disliked, avoiding uncomfortable situations, stereotyping... And yes, we are still communicating, because we are conveying information, but with what purpose?

If we dig deep, we'll discover that most of our communication problems are rooted in different shades of *fear*, that unpleasant emotion that we experience when we perceive a threat or danger. We fear what people will say and what people will think. We fear mistakes and failure. We want to be liked and accepted. We don't want to disappoint people or let them down. We don't want to upset others. We lack the confidence and resourcefulness to express ourselves... The list goes on. (This is the common tune I hear at each of my sessions.)

Communication is about the impact you make on the other person, and vice versa. But how can we have an impact when the premise that we operate from is one of fear? We are all different. We perceive reality from different perspectives; we possess different values, education and upbringing, which creates a huge gap that needs bridging. And at this point, we haven't yet added the international element – things get even more complex when you throw in cultural differences, languages and accents to the mix, creating a real international playground.

Into this playground, more leaders are being introduced every day. A big part of their success will depend on the quality of their communication, which in turn will dictate the quality of their relationships and, most importantly, their ability to motivate and positively influence people to drive business results. But how well equipped are these leaders to navigate the waters of human interactions, let alone the stormy international seas? How well equipped are *you*? The likely answer is that *there is room for improvement.* Would you agree?

As a leader, you must lead effectively, provide constructive feedback, challenge undesired behaviours, deal with conflict effectively, present your business and ideas in a compelling way, motivate, influence, coach, mentor and empower your people…

And it doesn't stop there. Let's add some more wood to this fire. The markets are getting more crowded and competition is fierce, so communicating, influencing and leading effectively is not enough. You need to be authentic to foster trust, relatability and understanding; your teams need to be more creative, resilient and flexible in the face of continuous change; a more daring mindset is needed to try new initiatives while embracing failure in the process, to eventually shine through and become the international business that is everything but vanilla. More than ever, you need to *stand out*.

If you've got this far, you might be thinking, 'Thank you, Jose, for painting this lovely picture and for all the encouragement.' I know it's grim – but it's also the reality. Can it be changed? Of course it can – that's why I decided to write this book on how you, as a leader, can simplify, improve and amplify your international impact through the power of positive influence.

This book is for leaders of international businesses and organisations who want to increase their ability to effectively lead individuals and teams who work across nations in order to improve productivity, morale, motivation, wellbeing, customer service, business relationships and more, to drive business results. If you are one of these leaders, continue reading.

What makes me the right person to write about this? I know what it's like to start from scratch (more than once), to move to a new country, to adapt to a new culture, to learn a new language, to develop and use my communication skills to move up the business ladder, to sell, to market products and services worldwide, to manage and lead teams and to run my own business. I speak to, train and coach people from a variety of countries and cultures on how to become impactful communicators. I've been working with global businesses and organisations as well as those who want to grow and expand internationally, for over ten years. I especially love working with organisations who need to engage with non-native English speakers, whether customers or teams, and don't possess the skills nor the awareness of how to effectively communicate across those boundaries.

I've been trusted by many top global companies, including SEAT and CUPRA (Volkswagen Group), Procter & Gamble and international organisations like the European Bank for Reconstruction and Development. Some of my articles have been featured on Yahoo Finance, Yahoo News, Mentors, Thrive Global, Disrupt Magazine, LA Weekly and The Influencer Age. I'm also a TEDx speaker and host, leadership and communication trainer, speaking coach, international business and marketing specialist, and founder of Jose Ucar Ltd. During the Covid-19 pandemic, I launched the World-Class Communicator online course to support people with their mindset and communication skills, and the community grew exponentially, reaching over forty thousand online students.

And I almost forgot, I also happen to be fluent in two of the most spoken languages in business worldwide, English and Spanish, which gives me a unique perspective when communicating internationally.

So that's me. But you might well be wondering, what does all this mean for you?

In this book, I will provide you with easy to grasp and apply concepts and frameworks that will enable you to thrive as a global business leader. I've divided this book into three parts. In the first, **Understanding Global Influence**, I cover topics such as the global playground, how to simplify your communication across nations, the core areas of global influence and its magnetic effect. In the second part, **Developing Your Global Influence**, I speak about authenticity and how to be less vanilla and essentially more you; the alienation game; how to increase your internationality (the heart of human connections across nations); the energy intensity in human interactions; the channels of global influence, and more. Finally, the third part, **Exercising Your Global Influence**, focuses on the importance of preparation, developing a fear-embracing mindset, the international behavioural styles analogy and how applying your global influence will impact your leadership, your people and your business growth and expansion. At the end of each chapter, you will also find some additional questions and actions to help you reflect on how you can apply the learnings from this book to your current situations and challenges.

I have based my work on the fact that it can take years to understand a culture and learn a language, but it can take only seconds to start building an authentic human connection. Thus, simplicity is key to improving and amplifying your global influence.

My wish for you is that, at the end of this book, you will be able to positively influence the people you lead by communicating effectively, with confidence and authenticity, in any scenario, whether internationally, virtually or even across your desk. You will be able to convey information with authority one-to-one and to an audience; will enhance your listening and questioning abilities to coach people using the shift framework; will deliver motivational and developmental feedback and engage in healthy conflict as and when required; and will never stop pursuing your goals while enabling others to achieve theirs.

Exercising global influence is not easy, and it won't happen overnight, but it is more than possible. It is also an extremely rewarding process once you commit yourself to being the best you can be daily. There is no secret, only a lot of focused work. Simply put, if this Venezuelan alien currently living in the UK can do it, so can you.

Let me show you how.

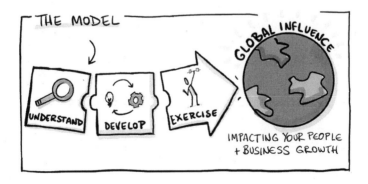

PART ONE
UNDERSTANDING GLOBAL INFLUENCE

As a business leader, understanding the concept of global influence is crucial to unleashing your full potential. Global influence goes beyond the ability to positively impact the individuals you work with; it involves creating a profound effect that extends across borders and cultures. By harnessing this power, you can initiate positive change not only within your organisation but also on a global scale.

In today's interconnected world, businesses operate in an increasingly borderless environment. The decisions you make and the actions you take can reverberate far beyond your immediate surroundings.

Understanding and exercising global influence is pivotal for business leaders seeking to create a lasting impact. By empowering individuals within your organisation and cultivating future leaders, you can spark a chain reaction that spreads wealth, opportunities and positive change worldwide.

ONE
It's All About Impact

In all our actions lies the power to influence others, and it is crucial that we embrace intentional positive impact. From the outset, I encourage you to challenge your thinking, as this book aims to magnify the effect you, as a business leader, can have on your people and, ultimately, your organisation's bottom line. By striving for positive outcomes, you can create a compound effect that ripples through every level of the business, fostering a culture of growth and success.

People

The foundation of your impact as a leader with global influence will always be people. You will create inner impact that will help them to become more authentic, increase their confidence and motivation, to name just a few benefits. From here, they will then go and interact with other members of the team and the organisation, clients, suppliers and wider stakeholders. Successful interactions can only happen through proactive and effective communication that encompasses an understanding of oneself and others. This is what will foster not good, but great relationships from which even greater business results will be achieved – higher productivity, better team morale and motivation, more sales, increased customer satisfaction, increased mental health and wellbeing... You will likely be able to think of even more benefits yourself.

The human explorer

A leader with global influence is a human explorer. Remember this: every human interaction is unique. To understand the link between being a human explorer and developing global influence, first we need to define global influence.

Global influence, as presented in this book, refers to the capacity to enable positive behavioural shifts in people. These positive shifts are attained by:

- Being authentic.

- Forging profound and enduring connections with individuals, irrespective of their cultural background, accent or country of origin.

- Adopting a holistic approach of conveying information effectively, providing coaching and challenging unhelpful behaviours, adapted to the unique needs and style of each individual.

To achieve the above, you need to regularly explore yourself to understand your weaknesses and strengths, your fears, confidence levels and any barriers or limitations that could be stopping you from being comfortable in your own skin, regardless of the external circumstances.

Next, you need to explore everything about the person or people you will be interacting with and how you feel about them and the situation. If I think about my most successful relationships, they've always involved a level of excitement and desire to engage and connect. Unfortunately, we often feel the opposite – we tend to get nervous and uncomfortable when we don't know exactly what's going to happen.

When you follow your excitement and curiosity about the human(s) in front of you, you will gain additional knowledge about how to best interact with them. Don't worry, I will provide you with frameworks and techniques that will increase your confidence and ability to adapt to any international scenario.

Finally, after gathering information about yourself and others, it's time to communicate in a way that creates impact. Remember this is happening within a business and leadership context, where you are articulating a message using of all of your body to get the receiver to consider their situation differently, reflect on it and, ideally, make a change for the better.

The learner and stretcher

A leader with global influence is also a learner and a stretcher. The learner part may make sense straight away. It's important that you search for new knowledge all the time because this is what will back you up when exploring and  delivering your impact. Read books, browse the internet and social media with purpose, look for coaches and mentors, surround yourself with people who will impact and boost your journey and ask them for help when you're stuck. Do these things intentionally and you will grow exponentially. Be hungry for knowledge and the application of it.

You can explore and be inquisitive, you can be a learner who applies the knowledge, but what will set you apart, what will make you *great* in terms of your global influence will be your stretching talent. Stretching refers to the act of challenging oneself and others to expand their capabilities, perspectives and boundaries.  It involves pushing beyond one's comfort zone, embracing discomfort, and taking risks to catalyse personal and global growth. Stretching talent encompasses the ability to inspire and encourage others to do the same, fostering a culture of continuous learning, innovation and positive change. In essence, stretching is about going beyond the ordinary and ordinary thinking to create a significant and transformative impact.

The global playground

When communicating with someone, you need to remember that your reality might be different to theirs.

I once started a virtual training session with the huge assumption that the people with their cameras turned off were not as interested and lacked confidence to show up. When delivering a session about communicating with impact and confidence to students from Latin America, Africa, Asia and Europe, I neglected to consider the possibility that some students could be having issues with a poor internet connection meaning they couldn't have the camera on. The amazing Sophie Daud from the Leaders Network kindly interrupted to highlight this. It hadn't crossed my mind. Yes, the international communicator and author of this book on global influence. Feel free to mock me a little bit.

The forex (foreign exchange) market serves as a pertinent analogy to describe the dynamics of the global playground because it is fluid, ever-changing and driven by emotions. While emotions play a significant role in both contexts, it is essential to recognise that the forex market is not solely driven by them. It is a complex marketplace influenced by many factors, including economic indicators, geopolitical events and market sentiment, as well as emotions.

The analogy applies to this dynamic global environment in the sense that each interaction is distinct, just as currency pairs behave uniquely in the forex market. When individuals from diverse backgrounds and perspectives converge, it is crucial to approach these interactions with presence, curiosity and a commitment to having a positive impact on the people or groups involved. Such an approach can set a constructive tone for various scenarios, including my virtual training session with the international group, by fostering understanding, empathy, collaboration and the exchange of valuable insights.

Looking at it from a different angle, I like to see people as equals in terms of their potential to achieve things in life, but do they see themselves under the same light? Communication is beautiful and it's an infinite game – it never stops, and the results are never definite. My concern had been that the cameras weren't off to excuse people from being fully present and dealing with their current fears and limitations.

We create our reality and tend to impose it onto others, mostly unconsciously. Now imagine how interesting things can get when different realities interact within an environment of people determined to achieve a worthwhile outcome. There lies the root of most of our communications challenges or learning opportunities, depending on how you choose to look at it. Our realities are being shaped from the moment we are born, from which point we are influenced by our cultures, language, music, education at home and school, and our experiences in life, both good and bad. What this does is build layers that separate us from our essence.

Can you guess what's coming next? Well, your mission as a Global Influence Leader is to remove these layers to communicate with the actual person behind them. A good analogy is of opening a door to enter that person's home. To do this, you need to find the key that will open the lock. But how can you find the key if you haven't left your own home yet? Linking it to the virtual session, I was too much in my own head from the start and didn't empathise with the audience as I could have done. In a way, I'm glad it happened, as now I won't repeat this mistake – and you are reading about it and hopefully learning from it.

Unlocking doors

The global playground is the environment in which we all operate. This is where we demonstrate our behaviours and show our reactions to what's happening at a certain moment in time. This is where all our realities collide. These are virtual realities, because they are all subjective – no one carries the ultimate truth. This is all happening at a superficial level. What you see here is a result of what's within the person. Remember the layers that cover our essence, who we really are? These are inspired by the work of Robert Dilts. Our persona in the global playground is the top, superficial layer.

But you want to access people's depths. You want to open the door to their home. At the next level, you tend to find that it's people's skills and knowledge that are driving behaviours and actions. Here lies what they know, and what they've learned and continue to learn. You want to become a better leader, so you learn about leadership. You want to become a better salsa dancer, so you go to Cali, Colombia (where my wife is from) and take some lessons. We learn new things to develop our competence, which in turn changes our conduct. This works most of the time. This is usually the level we tend to operate from when we have conversations with our team members and work colleagues. 'What skills would you like to develop?' is a common question in appraisals and personal development plans. Learning a language sits here – like any other skill, it involves practice, repetition, exposure and gradual improvement over time.

In the next layer down, is what we value and hold to be true. Here we find our culture, what we learned at home, in our country and from life and work experiences. This is the realm of self-empowerment and also self-limitation. Here is where we consciously or unconsciously decide what we can or can't do. What's acceptable and what isn't. Here we also find our moral compass, which guides us through all our human interactions telling us what's right and wrong.

Changes made here create a greater impact than those made at the skills and knowledge level. Why? Because as I like to say, it doesn't matter what or how much you know, but what you do with it. Despite possessing valuable knowledge, many individuals refrain from taking action due to various factors such as fear, limiting beliefs or lack of confidence. These barriers hinder their progress and potential for growth. By identifying and addressing these obstacles, you can help them unlock their true capabilities.

Finally, at the bottom level, you have your identity along with your big *why*, or reason for being. We don't tend to be conscious about who we are on a daily basis and how clarity (or lack thereof) on this impacts our results and how we come across. When writing this book, I'm channelling and presenting my knowledge through my global influence identity, and I'm very much connected to the reason behind this book.

Your team, clients and colleagues will generally present their situations at a superficial, external level. Your mission, or reason for existing, as a Global Influence Leader is to discover the internal elements that are causing them to act in the way they do and look to have a positive impact on their way of thinking, which in turn will transform their behaviour and results. Do they need new skills? Do they need to change some of their beliefs and values or perhaps to gain clarity on what they stand for and what drives them? The role of the global influence leader is to help others make changes at the different levels in order to impact their behaviours and results.

The international playground remains complex, but when it comes to human interactions within the scope of global influence, this multi-level framework provides areas of focus for you to unpick and drive change.

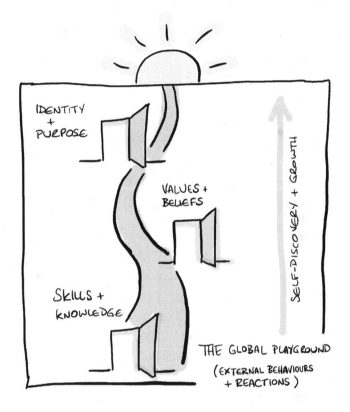

IDENTITY
+
PURPOSE

VALUES +
BELIEFS

SKILLS +
KNOWLEDGE

SELF-DISCOVERY + GROWTH

THE GLOBAL PLAYGROUND
(EXTERNAL BEHAVIOURS
+ REACTIONS)

Simplify your communication across nations

Above, I shared with you the global playground layers, to help you pinpoint the key levels people operate from internationally. This is important because, without knowing what to look for or pay attention to, we would be quite lost when trying to communicate in a way that can positively influence a team member or colleague.

According to the communication theory developed by Richard Bandler, we are exposed to billions of bits of information throughout the day. This information is filtered by the playground layers, creating our unique subjective reality. The mind then deletes, distorts and generalises this information in order to process more effectively what's happening in our surroundings. From this recreated reality we go and communicate, hence my favourite phrase: communication starts within.

You are in your own head every day and, let's be honest, it can get a little chaotic at times, to say the least. How can you be expected to communicate effectively with impact, to influence? This is why some individuals may appear to be poor communicators: not listening well, speaking rapidly, being indirect, staying silent, lacking empathy or showing an abundance of it, being overly straightforward or highly analytical and using unfamiliar words.

Many of the problems that arise in life are linked to communication, either with another person, a group of people or even with yourself. These issues can be influenced by your perception of specific situations, impacting how you navigate and address them.

The solution I'm going to present here is *simpler* than you might expect. Pun intended. Based on what we've covered so far, it's crucial to chart a clear path for direction and intention. As aspiring leaders with global influence, simplifying your international communication is essential, especially considering the complexities we often encounter in our minds, let alone when communicating across nations.

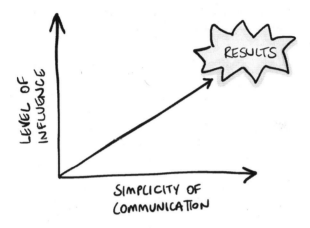

According to the International Labor Union, 70% of global ventures fail due to cultural differences (Thought Farmer, 2014). Aon Hewitt's 2011 study found that 33% of participants attributed deal failures to 'cultural integration issues'. Similarly, in a study by Marsh Mercer Kroll, 50% of respondents identified 'organisational cultural differences' as the key post-deal challenge (Carpenter and Wyman, 2008). These findings underline the significance of effective and simplified cross-cultural communication in increasing influence and achieving greater results.

The SIMPLER acronym stands for:

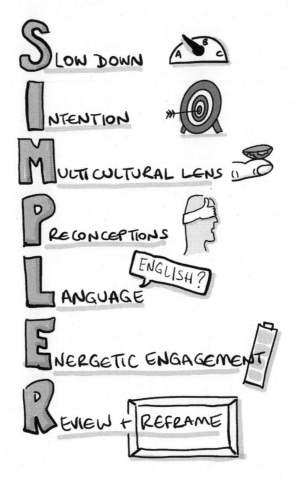

Let's look at each step in more detail.

Slow down

This is one of the most important steps, hence it's the first. You need to slow down your thinking and take time to formulate what you want to say based on the person and situation in front of you. Especially in a business environment, aim to be:

- Accurate – convey information that is correct

- Brief – be efficient with your words

- Clear – make sure people understand

Intention

When you slow down, this will give you space. Use this to think about the impact you want to make or the result you would like to achieve after the communication has taken place. The I also stands for 'I' as in *you*. You are the person in charge of the process. If the outcome is not what you expected, you need to review and/or reframe (the final step in the SIMPLER method).

Multicultural lens

Start seeing your interactions through a broader lens, not expecting to know all the intricacies of every culture but being accepting and respectful of all the differences you perceive while also looking for similarities. Pay attention to what makes people tick, be curious and ask questions.

Be mindful of blind spots, which can still influence your perception, even with the best intentions (as my assumption about the switched off cameras showed). Acknowledging your own limitations and biases is a crucial step in developing a multicultural perspective. When you encounter unfamiliar customs or beliefs, approach them with humility and a willingness to learn.

Preconceptions

As explained earlier, our experiences in life have led us to form beliefs, values and opinions on events and people. My wife hates it when she meets people who bring up the drugs conversation or mention Pablo Escobar just because she is Colombian, or when people assume that I'm a good dancer because I was raised by the Caribbean Sea. In this latter case, it's true and I don't mind, but my point is that we are all unique, so focus on the person and be open to creating more informed conceptions.

Language

Since English is the most spoken language in business worldwide, I'm assuming that the people you communicate with will be either a native or a non-native

English speaker. If it's the latter, pay attention to their proficiency level and be mindful of the use of slang, common sayings and other colloquial expressions. As a rule of thumb (there's one!), keep it simple and gauge the person's level of understanding without appearing patronising. I left my first business meeting in the UK back in 2007 feeling quite overwhelmed because I'd only managed to understand a small portion of what was shared. Adapt your language and check their level of understanding. This also applies to native speakers from different countries, and those from the same country. In communication, less tends to be more, and simplicity can increase your influence when communicating internationally.

Energetic engagement

I just love this. People always say to me that they like my energy and engagement. I may have learned it from my grandad, who enjoyed talking to anyone and always managed to put a smile on their faces. We feel people's energy and it helps us connect with them. Even before we say a word, our energy and presence have strongly influenced how we are being perceived by others. Remember that communication starts within, so be mindful of the thoughts you carry and inject some excitement when meeting anyone. Always be appreciative, respectful, humble and humorous and you will notice a change in your relationships. Think about how you can leave that person better off after interacting with you.

Review and reframe

Following an interaction, take some time to think about how it went and whether you could have done anything differently. This proactive habit of looking at things in hindsight will support you in developing your global influence. In cases where the communication is not working for you, reframing will help you to find new perspectives and resources. When you reframe a situation, you change the meaning you've given to it, to something that serves you and the relationship better. Here is an example of a simple and quick reframe. When I lived in Spain, it used to annoy me when people asked me where I was from, because I found it intrusive. To reframe this annoyance, I simply asked myself the question, 'What else could this mean?' The answer that came to mind was, 'You speak differently, and they find you interesting.' Voila! A better perspective.

CASE STORY – 'JOSE, I CAN'T PUT MYSELF OUT THERE'

During a training session I was delivering to an international group of leaders, it became apparent that one of the participants was struggling to put herself out there. This led to a coaching session to explore the issue further.

Stephanie, a talented and accomplished professional of Polish origin and currently working for a global firm, conveyed that she was having difficulties presenting her ideas openly in meetings and other business situations.

This was the external or superficial problem that she was presenting to me. There are different valid approaches to deal with this situation, but let's look at how I went about uncovering the various layers to support a highly capable businesswoman to shine in her corporate role.

Knowing from previous conversations we'd had that she was more than able to share her ideas, and that she had received plenty of training on communication and presentation skills, I decided to go straight for a deeper door sitting at the identity level and tried to unlock it.

ME: Steph, tell me. What do you believe about yourself?

STEPHANIE: Jose, I believe that I'm not good enough.

ME: When did you decide this?

STEPHANIE: I'm not sure. I think it comes from my childhood. My ideas were never heard by my father.

ME: Who are you in this situation with your father?

STEPHANIE: Well, I'm a little girl.

JOSE: Who are you at work?

STEPHANIE: I often feel like that little girl.

JOSE: Right now, who would you like to be instead?

STEPHANIE: I'd like to be a capable businesswoman who can achieve anything she sets her mind to.

JOSE: Isn't that who you already are?

STEPHANIE: Yes, that's who I am.

JOSE: Tell me, why are you here?

STEPHANIE: I want to drive change and support women within this organisation.

JOSE: With this clarity and understanding of who you are and why you are here, can you now put yourself out there?

STEPHANIE: Yes, nothing can hold my voice back. These women are counting on me.

In this case story, Stephanie was connecting with her childhood identity at work, which wasn't supporting the results she wanted to achieve. Gaining clarity about her identity and purpose created a positive shift in her state of mind and behaviour.

 Help the people you lead to shift their behaviours by unlocking some of their doors.

Self-reflection

The time you spend on the Self-reflection and Action points sections of each chapter is entirely up to you. I usually recommend at least five minutes to consider the questions and set some intentions moving forward.

- How well are you embracing intentional positive impact in your leadership role?

- Are you truly exploring and understanding yourself, as well as the individuals you interact with?

- In what ways are you demonstrating a commitment to continuous learning and growth?

- How comfortable are you with stepping out of your comfort zone to stretch yourself and others?

- Are you effectively simplifying your cross-cultural communication to enhance your global influence?

Action points

- Invest in your global influence to increase your authenticity and success in business relationships.

- Position yourself as a leader who can make a meaningful impact across situations and cultures.

- Embrace the global playground by acknowledging the uniqueness of every human interaction.

- Stay present and maintain curiosity in your international engagements.

- Recognise that it can be SIMPLER than you perceive.

- Be proactive in your thinking to regulate emotions and respond effectively in any situation.

TWO

The Three Core Areas Of Global Influence

M y international travels started in 1998, when
I was sixteen years old. Back then, I knew little
about the impact international human connections
were going to have in my life. It's not always easy to
learn a new language, adapt to a different culture and
make friends, so as you can imagine, I struggled at
first. But as I got more comfortable and confident navigating through my new environment, things started
to improve.

This was my process in Sweden, Spain, the USA and
in the UK, where I live now. These moves occurred
at different stages in my life, but my behavioural
patterns and learning curves were pretty consistent.
While living in these countries, especially Spain and

the UK, I had the opportunity to do a lot of travelling for business. First, I was in charge of supporting Spanish companies to develop their internationalisation strategies. Then I was hired by an engineering business near London where I wore a lot of hats; towards the end I did sales, and I finished as EU marketing manager.

That is a short version of the story and I'm sharing it because, over a period of around ten years, I worked and did business with multiple people from various backgrounds and nationalities. On top of that, I can add at least six consecutive years when I've been coaching, training and speaking on communication, confidence, resilience and leadership.

From these experiences, what I realised is that the most successful moments of my business career have been those where I've been in complete alignment. Moments when my mind, heart and body have been in total harmony. These have been my moments of genius, flow, elevated synchronicity – however you want to label them. It's been the same with my personal relationships. This is the reason why I created a process within this book to help you simplify, improve and amplify your international impact in any setting. To achieve this, you need to understand the core areas of global influence: the interconnected realms of heart, mind and body.

Heart

The heart is the very core of our existence, as it is the place from which all our emotions stem. Emotions are an integral part of being human, regardless of whether we outwardly express them or keep them hidden.

Reflecting and analysing, in hindsight, I realised that each of my successful relationships since I started travelling has something in common. They all have heart. The most amazing ones have a pure, raw heart, here I place my relationships with my parents, grandparents, wife, Swedish families and some of my best friends. There is great value in this realisation, because often we suppress our feelings due to fear, cultural norms and other societal conventions.

To be an outstanding leader with global influence, it's vital that you become more aware of your feelings and learn to use them in your human interactions. You can do this by giving others the gift of your undivided attention and engaging in heartfelt communication.

Giving someone your undivided attention means being present for that person, or for your audience. It means being empathetic, vulnerable, excited, in tune with your feelings and those of the other party. It means listening with all of your senses, being in the moment while enjoying the essence of the human being in front of you. This is how you start creating impact and positively influencing the people around you. Put their heart and needs before yours, explore and enjoy.

When delving into heartfelt communication, it's crucial to consider the role our emotions play throughout the process, as they can be a help or a hindrance.

When feelings get in the way

Let's take a common example that most people can relate to. When you have an argument with someone, you can be so overwhelmed by feelings that you end up saying things you may later regret. Or the complete opposite can occur, where your feelings prevent you from saying something that could have made a positive difference to the situation.

Our feelings can also get in the way when we present in public, when we come into a new environment, when providing feedback to our team members, saying no to a client, being assertive, handling conflict, standing by our decisions, dealing with failure and so on.

These situations can lead us to shut down our feelings because they are uncomfortable, because they might show weakness and because we don't want to be perceived as not being in control or as not knowing what we are doing (which is perfectly normal, by the way, and happens to all of us). If you continue down this path, building up metaphorical walls to hide behind, not dealing with these emotions, bottling them up, how you do expect to lead people to reach their potential and influence others? By holding yourself back, you are holding them back.

But hey, there is always another way. In fact, there are many other ways to go about this.

When feelings pave our way

When we allow our feelings to pave the way, this is when our energy shines and we can impact people. Still, additional channelling is required for greater impact and transformation, which we will cover in the following chapters, but let's focus on the heart for now.

When we give people our undivided attention, an invisible bond is created, one which is real and authentic. This bond is the human connection being established and its intensity and duration will depend on how we balance our heart with our mind and body. You know when you see a person, and you don't know what it is, but there is just something you like about them? This is a pure heart connection in the making. While this connection might not necessarily develop further, I encourage you to acknowledge and appreciate the feeling.

Our emotions can hold us back, as we have discussed, but if we understand them and use them to grow and to deal with difficult situations and challenges, we can achieve incredible things. We feel fear a lot of the time, but we can always use it to our benefit and the benefit of the people within our tribe.

Consider this: I'm your manager, and I notice something about your behaviour that I believe you could change to increase your influence. I don't tell you because I'm afraid of your reaction, or because I don't want to upset you. I don't want you to reject my opinion. Deep inside, I want to be liked and accepted, and so, ultimately, I don't say anything. The behaviour I've noticed in you is a lack of empathy and listening skills, which are fundamental for effective communication. By not dealing with my own emotions, I'm doing you a disservice. My fear of failure is hindering your development.

The heart tells us what to do and the mind, by applying its filters, rationalises the scenario with the ultimate goal of protecting us from the things we fear. Well, it's time to change this. How? By taking the first step. Find a way to say what you feel and embrace whatever response you receive.

If you've ever overcome any type of fear in your life, you will know how great it feels to be on the other side. Remember this the next time fear threatens to stop you from sharing what you feel.

Make fear your friend and always listen to your heart.

But using your heart alone is not enough; this is where the mind and body come in.

Mind

The 'mind' element of the model pertains to the rational and analytical aspect of communication. It is where we engage in decision-making, strategic planning, envisioning outcomes, setting intentions, following up on tasks and applying the frameworks provided in this book, among other practices.

The brain's role in regulating emotions and actions is crucial to understand, and while this idea may not be groundbreaking, it remains highly relevant. By developing awareness of how your rational thinking influences how you feel and what you do, you gain the power to effect positive change in your relationships.

You need to be in charge, or someone else will. Remember back in chapter one when I said that you are in charge of your communication? Well, you can't control the other person, but you can definitely influence them towards your intended outcome. This is the ideal scenario, but what about all the situations where something has happened or someone said something to you and you reacted defensively, misread the situation, felt let down, blamed them for your feelings, got hurt, went and complained behind their back...? All of these examples represent situations where you weren't in control of yourself and unconsciously gave someone else the power to negatively influence you. They were then in charge of your thinking, feelings and actions, not you. This happens when you are reactive instead of proactive.

To enhance and strengthen your global influence, you must cultivate control over your thoughts and emotions. By consistently exercising this skill, you will find yourself capable of maintaining a more calm and focused state of mind, irrespective of the context you operate in, ultimately increasing your overall influence and effectiveness.

Drawing a rational line

Here is a simple two-step technique you can use to start turning these negative situations around, which will also improve the relationship with the other person.

1. Whatever the negative feeling, ask yourself, 'Do I like feeling this way?' Unless you want to remain a victim of the circumstances, you'll probably say 'no'.

2. Follow this with another question: 'How do I *want* to feel now?' Or, 'What's a more

resourceful state for me to be in, to have a positive impact on this relationship?'

This is what I call drawing a rational line – interrupting your feelings in a logical and proactive fashion. Try it next time your emotions take over.

It's important, though, not to get *too* rational. By this I mean you should remain in control, but don't overdo it to the point you that suppress your emotions. The risk is that you get stuck in your own head, begin to overthink and stop taking action or making decisions – this will reduce your influence and impact on others.

What you're trying to do is reach a balance between heart, mind and body. If you lead by heart only, your interactions may be too emotional and lack the subtleties a trained mind can deliver, but too much mind can create barriers to heartfelt connections.

During my career I've met so many incredible people, and lots of them struggled with their mind getting in the way of their ability to communicate freely, openly and authentically. They were always wondering, 'What if?' and it stopped them from taking actions. But, what if it works? What if it gives you unexpected but positive results? 'What if' can also be framed with an optimistic outlook.

I have many clients who are incredible entrepreneurs, business owners and leaders, but who I have told on a few occasions that they can come across as autocratic. A more powerful way to be than autocratic would be charismatic – a sweet balance between being approachable and credible. The kind of leader that people can open up to and whom they also respect a great deal. To make this change, they need to increase their vulnerability – or, to use the terms of this book, by injecting more heart into their communications, they can take their relationships to a whole new level.

To let your mind's guards down and let go, you must gently navigate your fears. Confront the difficult moments – times of hurt, bullying, feeling inadequate, facing prejudice, enduring hurtful names and being undermined. Approach these experiences with care and compassion as you embark on this journey. Allow your mind to embrace the rollercoaster of emotions, to process, heal and, ultimately, find strength and growth.

 Teach your mind to influence you so that you can influence others.

Body

The third, but no less important element, is the body. This is the action, behaviours or materialisation of heart and mind. The body is what will enable us to convey what we carry inside and unleash our excellence.

The concept of the body element encompasses a range of communicative aspects, including both written and spoken language, tonality and physiology. It's the tangible and observable part of communication; it's the outward manifestation that you encounter when interacting with others. This physical aspect serves as a mirror, reflecting the inner workings of the mind and heart.

The way someone carries themselves, their gestures, facial expressions and even the nuances of their speech, can offer profound insights into their thoughts, emotions and intentions. This nonverbal language often communicates more than words alone. By keenly observing these cues, you gain access to a wealth of information that can be harnessed to influence people positively. Understanding and interpreting the body allows you to read between the lines, comprehend unspoken sentiments and forge deeper connections. By recognising the intricate connections between the heart, mind and body, you unlock the potential to communicate more effectively and make a meaningful impact on those around you.

Let's look at the four levels of acting, the bodily manifestations of heart and mind:

- Mind acting (mind–body)
- Heart acting (heart–body)
- Inacting (no body)
- Heart–mind acting (heart–mind–body)

47

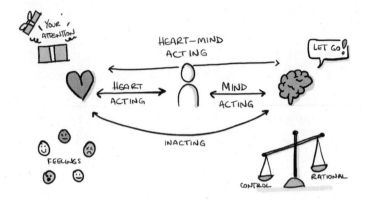

Mind acting

This occurs when the mind is in charge. When we communicate with others from this level, they may perceive us in different ways.

Forward mind. This is when the mind overrides emotions and conveys a unilateral message without considering the heart of the person  or audience you are communicating with. This can be perceived as authoritative, insensitive, arrogant, very direct, aggressive and overconfident. Many strong leaders can operate from this level.

Withdrawn mind. Again, the mind overrides what you feel but, in this case, it stops or slows down your action. We fall into this category when we overthink, second-guess ourselves and fixate on the problem or the negative outcomes of our communication. Operating at this level, a person can be perceived as thoughtful and credible but also passive, timid, insecure and lacking in confidence. Here you may find the clever individuals who love numbers and enjoy solving complex problems.

Operating solely from one of these levels can limit your influence. As human beings, we also need to engage the heart.

Heart acting

This is the opposite of mind acting. This is the realm of showing feelings and emotions and, depending on the levels of intensity at which they do this, I divide these behaviours into two categories:

Excited heart. People in this category freely unleash their emotions to the world. They are extremely captivating, creative and inspiring. There  can be too much telling, on occasion, without enough meaningful content. They crave human connection and ongoing recognition. People acting from this level can be perceived as too emotional, excitable and loud, but also energetic, engaging and confident. You often find those individuals with a tendency towards excited hearts in the creative industries.

Caring heart. This is exactly what it says on the tin. The caring heart cares for other people. It's not about showing emotions to the world but receiving them. These are extremely likeable people; they are empathetic and always looking to serve and support. They put others before themselves and are generally the people you turn to when you have a problem. You often find individuals with a tendency towards caring hearts in human resources and health and care services positions. They are perceived as approachable, are generally quiet and don't enjoy confrontation, and might show a lack of confidence in their demeanour, which may not necessarily be accurate. I also describe these people as 'relaxed hearts'.

In either case, exclusively relying on the above behaviours can constrain your ability to influence. The cognitive power of the mind also plays an essential role.

Inacting

'Inacting' is a made-up word to refer to a lack of action. This happens when our heart speaks to us, then the mind rationalises the heck out of it and we end up taking no action at all (no body), which, in this context, means we don't communicate.

Have you ever been in a meeting with an idea to share but you hold back, and then someone else comes up with it? This is a clear example of inaction. Bear in mind that though you may not say a word, your body will still speak for you. We are always communicating.

I suggest that you move away from inacting, because it's stopping you from gaining valuable feedback from the communication process. Feedback is a great source of learning. And who knows, maybe that's the idea that could lead to a promotion or unexpected new opportunities.

 All feedback can be good feedback. If you remain open, you may be able to learn something.

Heart-mind acting

 Picture this as the melting pot of the above levels of bodily manifestation. You may have found that you've identified more with one level so far, and that is normal. My aim is that, after recognising this, you will move onto thinking about how you can gain further malleability – how you can shape your heart–mind–body to be able to magnify your influence.

This is where our feelings, channelled through our minds, expressed through our body and adapted to the person in front of us, will have the greatest impact. This is channelled energy for global influence. This is the foundation for successful relationships with people in your business, city, country or across nations.

CASE STORY – 'JOSE, I'M BEING PERCEIVED AS ARROGANT!'

Matt was a delegate at one of my leadership and impactful communication sessions. He was a manager at a large multinational and, I have to say, was a clever young man, with a strong presence and great voice projection. His contributions were valid, but I sensed something off about him. I didn't know what it was initially, but I was struggling to create a connection with him. With assertiveness and openness to healthy conflict being one of my values, at some point I managed to have a conversation with him away from the group and I shared my feelings. I conveyed to him that on occasion he came across as arrogant and his response was, 'Yes, I've been told that before.' That was pretty much the end of the conversation, but here comes the interesting part. Two weeks later, during our scheduled one-to-one coaching, he decided to explore his arrogance. My words had hit a nerve.

During that conversation, it became obvious that he was mainly operating from a forward mind level. He had his reasons for this, but I could feel that he was suppressing some of his emotions. As he began to open up, he started to show more of his caring heart, which was amazing to see. It was a moment of vulnerability that completely changed my perception of him.

Some of the actions agreed at the end of the session were that he would be more self-aware of his behaviours and would pay attention to how he was being perceived by others, and consider the impact this would have on his leadership.

I'm delighted to share that, during our last meeting, being in Matt's presence was truly enjoyable – he even gave me a gift. Most importantly, his leadership style has evolved to become more approachable, and his team is responding positively to the change.

There are two main points to this story. First, I decided to be forward and caring with him when I expressed what my perception of him had been. Share your thoughts and feelings with your teams and create a space for them to share theirs. Second, be mindful of how you are being perceived and the influence it may have on the people you lead.

You can impact people's perception of you by proactively changing some of your behaviours.

Self-reflection

- How have you allowed fear, societal conventions, or cultural influences to affect your ability to express your genuine emotions in both personal and professional relationships?

- In what situations have you let your rational thinking override your emotions, leading to missed opportunities for deeper connections or positive influence?

- How do you currently convey your thoughts, emotions and intentions through your nonverbal communication (gestures, tone, posture)? Are there areas where you could align your body language more effectively with your heart and mind?

- Can you recall a specific instance where you successfully balanced your heart and mind, and effectively conveyed your emotions while maintaining a rational approach? What factors contributed to this success?

- Are there times when you've held back from communicating your thoughts or feelings due to overthinking or fear? How has this inaction impacted your relationships and potential for influence?

Action points

- Practise the skill of connecting heart, mind and body in your communication.

- Craft messages that resonate emotionally and intellectually, and that motivate action.

- Learn to gauge when your communication is overly heart-centred and adjust it to suit the context.

- Similarly, infuse more heart into communication that leans too heavily to the analytical side.

- Embrace action, dare to make mistakes and recognise them as valuable feedback and opportunities for personal and leadership growth.

- Cultivate adaptability as a leader, remaining flexible and open to change.

- Continuously adjust your approach to better connect with and influence others.

THREE

The Magnetic Effect Of Global Influence

In this chapter, I want to explore with you the magnetic effect of influence that unfolds when you embrace the synergy of mind, body and heart within the international playground.

The convergence of these three core areas forms the essence of a transformative force that sets the stage for remarkable change and influence. When you operate from a place of logic and mindful awareness (mind), energetic and vital intended action (body) and genuine compassion and excitement (heart), you tap into a unique and compelling power that will impact human growth, foster valuable connections and trigger unforeseen ripples that will greatly enrich both your business and personal life.

Let's dive right in.

Human growth: The unlimited expansion

I'm here today not just because I've worked tirelessly and have consistently stayed on track; I'm here today because of the amazing people in my life. I'm in the UK because of one person. His name is Alan Pearce, and I want to share part of our story to bring this section to life. This is not about my global influence, it's about Alan's.

I met Alan in Spain during the World-Cutting Tool Conference organised in San Sebastian, Spain, back in 2007. In less than an hour, while travelling on a bus from San Sebastian to Bilbao, he connected with me in such a way that I immediately looked up to him (yes, it was love at first sight). Seriously, at that precise moment he managed to find out enough information about me, my motivations and goals, to formulate a quick plan that could potentially work for me. He shared his idea and I said yes. It was fairly simple. That moment changed my life forever: three months later, I was working in Wokingham, a small town in Berkshire, UK. Alan, with his cockney English accent, and Jose, with his not so advanced Venezuelan-American accent, developed a relationship that still stands strong today. When I say that it may take years to learn a language and a culture, but it can take just seconds to build a strong human connection, this is what I mean. Here you have it – the proof is in the pudding (if I translate that into Spanish it makes no sense, by the way).

When you invest in developing your global influence, this is the kind of change you can create. Unlimited human expansion that initiates a powerful compound effect. Alan elevated me and now I'm hoping to elevate you, and so the magnetism continues. Alan is a great example of a leader with global influence. He is also extremely authentic, a topic that we will cover later in this book.

The shift through power

Remember the explorer, learner and stretcher from chapter one? By being curious and inquisitive, learning all you can about the other person and looking for where you can stretch yourself is a powerful way to lead with global influence. The intention behind influence is that you trigger a shift in something in the person's heart (feelings), mind (thought process) and/or body (actions).

Developing the core areas of your global influence will give you the POWER to help others grow. Alan has got his own version of power. Not the, 'I've got the power and you will submit to my command' kind, but something more like this:

- **Pathfinder:** Through your actions and results, you will become a guiding light for your team and circle of people. The person they come to for help finding solutions. The person to show them that there can be another way. The person with the answers and a fresh outlook. The person with clarity. The person with the business and life compass.

- **Openness:** Like a book, you've got nothing to hide, because you are always doing the work to improve as a person, leader and communicator. You understand how important it is to be vulnerable and authentic. You admit your mistakes and apologise when you need to. We tend to wear different masks as a consequence of our fifty shades of fear, but through openness you will show your true self in order to connect with another self.

- **Willingness:** We all have bad days, but regardless, you are willing to put whatever you are going through to one side in order to support your people. This willingness also presents as a desire to help by putting yourself forward when you feel people might need you. You are ready to go. People can count on you.

- **Elevate:** You always leave people better off. Dale Carnegie argues in his book, *How to Make Friends and Influence People*, that there are no neutral interactions. You either build people up or tear them down. You are the one building people up, always taking them to new heights and making them better. Even if this means challenging them and not agreeing with their views. This is about doing what you believe is right to help them grow.

- **Rapport:** This is your ability to create a harmonious relationship with the people you interact with. Being able to create almost instant rapport will help others to open up to you. The skill of making people feel at ease, combined with your pathfinder role, your openness, your willingness to support and your intention to help others improve, will mean that people trust you, respect you and believe in you. Now that is powerful.

This power will help build your credibility and approachability as a leader. You want people to follow you because they identify with you, respect you, look up to you, can learn from you, be themselves, express their feelings, share their problems and expect a shift. They know they can come to you because you've got POWER.

 Real global influence is not imposed, it is earned.
Are you ready to develop your power?

Valuable relationships

I can write a long list of all the people who have positively impacted my life, and I'm sure you can too.
But in this part of the book, I want to focus on the

ingredients that made these relationships so great, because that is one of the aims of your global influence – to attract and develop meaningful relationships. Those relationships that may not necessarily be measured in terms of longevity, because people come and go, but that leave a certain mark. Relationships that teach you something, that challenge you, that make you better.

As you embrace the concepts that I share in this book and your influence improves and amplifies, you will begin to build relationships that give you incredible value because they will be based around trust. The magic ingredient to the relationship salsa is trust.

In his book *The Five Dysfunctions of a Team*, Patrick Lencioni names the absence of trust as the first element that gets in the way of building high-performing teams. I don't think you are reading this book and putting up with my writing because you want to be an average leader with an average team that achieves average results. Of course not; you want to create ripples that transcend nations. So let's talk about trust.

To explain my concept of trust, I need to begin with a story of me eating tacos in Mexico City. I find that the best way to understand a culture and connect with people is by trying their food at their local place. It's like a deep dive into their values, customs and styles of communication. It gives you a quick yet in-depth understanding about who they are and how they operate. On all the business trips I've taken, I've consistently requested to dine at local places. I've also frequently had the delightful opportunity of being invited to share meals with my clients, business partners and team members in their homes, where I've been able to meet their families.

Back to my taco story. I was travelling with two Mexican colleagues and I was starving, because I didn't want to eat at the hotel. So I asked them, 'Where do you guys find the best tacos in town?' Being Venezuelan, I know how delicious proper street food can be. They ended up taking me to this place where they made tacos al pastor: slices of marinated pork on top of a tortilla with sliced onions, cilantro and their secret salsa. The tacos felt as if they were made especially for me and, in a way, they were, because I was chatting with the cook right there on the street who was asking what I wanted on my tacos, while enjoying some human authenticity along with candour, humour and a strong sense of positivity. There were no masks, just human beings sharing a fun experience around food.

After that day, I realised that if you want to build trust in your relationships, all you need to do is to go and eat a taco with that person. What do I mean? To build trust, you need: tailoring, authenticity, candour and optimism – TACO.

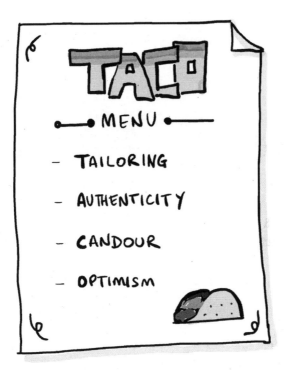

Let me break it down:

- **Tailoring:** Tailor your approach to the other person. Picture yourself making that taco just how the other person likes it. To positively influence another person, think about the impact you want to create for them and adapt your heart, mind and body accordingly. To paraphrase Dale Carnegie: if you want to influence others, you can either be yourself or change yourself. You remain yourself but adapt your behaviour to suit the current interaction. This will make the person feel at ease and encourage them to open up.

- **Authenticity:** Just be you, open and vulnerable. Embrace your uniqueness, because everyone else is taken. Be like the cook at the taco place, who wasn't trying to do anything fancy, and enjoy being comfortable in your own skin. This will help you bring down any internal barriers you had up while increasing your confidence and ability to connect with others. People respect the certainty that comes from this, even if they don't agree with it.

- **Candour:** At the taco place, people from different walks of life, whether rich or poor, from lawyers to taxi drivers, would converge to enjoy the same great food while briefly engaging with each other. I didn't notice any taboos or defensive behaviours; no aggression, no pretension, just people being people. I felt honesty and transparency, which are fundamental to developing trust with others. The cooks would challenge each other and clients with humour, the kind of confrontation that builds bridges. Being candid is so important, yet people can struggle to communicate with frankness.

- **Optimism:** It's interesting when I think back to how uplifted I felt after spending half an hour of my day at that place. The food was amazing; my belly was full and so was my heart. A combination of humour, positivity and fun can create long-lasting memories and will certainly develop a level of trust. This is what happened to me back in 2008.

I don't remember the name of the taco place nor its location within one of the largest cities in the world, but the memory of the experience will stay with me forever. You can be this person, the one who people will always remember because of how you made them feel. Having a more positive outlook towards situations will improve your performance and well-being and have a magnetic effect on those you lead.

Next time you travel for work or find yourself in a new city, ask the people you are with to take you to their most iconic food joint and enjoy the magic that will unfold. Go and eat a taco (or several of them), enjoy an arepa (a cornmeal cake eaten in parts of Central and South America), drink a Turkish coffee, have fika with your Swedish colleagues, a pad thai on a banana leaf, a Bombay sandwich in India, a talo with txistorra in the Basque Country. Get interested in people's countries, cultures and backgrounds, get involved and notice how they appreciate and respect you for it. At the same time, you will learn a great deal about them – remember, you are an explorer and a learner, and trust is key to being a stretcher.

Magic

Think of magic as the unexpected, all those things that happen in your life that you didn't account nor plan for. Some of us call it luck. I personally believe that luck tends to happen when you do the work, so I prefer the word 'magic'. But it's not only about the work; it's about the passion, the desire to discover and improve, guided by a strong vision. This vision can be short or long term, but it needs to strongly resonate with you. So we have:

Magic = Hard and Consistent Work +
Passion + Vision

But allow me to expand on this formula. When I was five years old, I said to my mum that I wanted to be international. I held onto that desire, and by the age of sixteen I was travelling to Sweden as an exchange student. The real magic at play here was that my parents re-mortgaged our house to pay for the trip. A few months after I left, my mum fell very sick. In Venezuela, social security is not something we are proud of. They found themselves with no money for them, let alone to support me abroad. My grandad's brother, Humberto, stepped in and lent them money; my godmother (though never formalised), Merche, started sending me money to cover some of my expenses; and my dad started making pan de jamón (typical Venezuelan Christmas food) over the festive period to send me more money. My Swedish host families took care of me as if I was their own child.

My own input back then was minimal. I studied and prepared to secure my slot within the exchange student programme and placed twenty-seventh out of over 300 students. In Sweden, I adapted by learning the culture and the language. But everything else was down to the magic created by the people in my circle. So my updated magic formula would look something like this:

$$\text{MAGIC} = \text{HARD + CONSISTENT WORK} + \text{PASSION} + \text{VISION} + \text{PEOPLE}$$

As I grew up, my input grew in terms of the work, the passion and the vision, but still, without those people I wouldn't be where I am today. My success in life up to this point has been due to that same magic formula. I took the long road here to highlight the importance of what you do as a leader because you are a catalyst for the magic of your people, just as they are for you. You trigger magic for them when you go the extra mile to support, believe in and develop them. You give them direction, prioritise their best interest over your own and show unconditional commitment to creating positive impact in their careers and life. Without expecting anything in return, they will impact your magic in ways you would never imagine.

 People are part of your magic, and you are part of theirs.

CASE STORY – 'JOSE, I WANT TO BE MORE CANDID!'

Mark is a highly skilled and knowledgeable leader. He is also an amazing person with whom I developed a quick and strong connection at a training session I delivered. One of the behaviours we worked on together was his ability to be more candid in his communication. We used role play to explore this and uncover what could potentially be hindering him. He is a likeable person who doesn't want to upset others and, underneath that, like many of us (including myself) he wanted to be accepted and liked. Two weeks after the session, during a coaching meeting, he mentioned that he had been consciously trying to be clearer and more direct in his communication by getting straight to the point instead of beating around the bush. He noted that his communication with one of his direct reports was improving, which he attributed to his proactive engagement and more regular directiveness.

Mark also shared that he was coaching his son's football team and that this behavioural shift (being more candid) was already creating ripples amongst parents, as he'd asked them to be more involved in their children's diets and fitness in order to improve their performance on the field but also, and most importantly, their health. This is a great case of magic in action.

See? There is no luck, just the compound effect of your directed actions. Trust the magic of your global influence.

Self-reflection

- How can you enhance your ability to impact human growth and connections at an international level?

- How can you become a more authentic and compassionate leader who fosters meaningful connections and creates a positive ripple effect?

- Are you willing to embrace the qualities of a leader with global influence and power, such as being a Pathfinder, cultivating Openness, demonstrating Willingness, consistently Elevating others, and building Rapport? How can you actively develop these qualities in your interactions?

- In building valuable relationships that are based on trust, how can you Tailor your approach to others, be more Authentic, practise Candour, and infuse Optimism into your interactions to create a stronger foundation of connection and influence?

- How can you combine hard and consistent work, passion, vision and positive impact on other people to create magic in your leadership approach?

Action points

- Recognise the potential of global influence to foster human growth.

- Understand the significant impact you can bring through your leadership.

- Cultivate your POWER by developing your individual strengths and capabilities.

- Focus on nurturing and upholding the trust of the remarkable individuals under your leadership by applying the TACO framework.

- Engage in consistent, passionate effort, guided by a clear vision.

- Strive to make a positive impact on people's lives, consistently and optimistically.

PART TWO
DEVELOPING YOUR
GLOBAL INFLUENCE

The second part of this book represents the next stage of the Global Influence Model, where you will learn how you can become more authentic by nurturing a unique way of thinking that will make you stand out in your own way while fully trusting who you are. You will expand your understanding of what I call internationality, the heart of international human interactions. Finally, we'll cover the channels of global influence, where I will show you how to communicate to positively impact almost anyone.

Shall we?

FOUR
Authenticity

Being authentic has brought incredible opportunities into my life, from coaching multimillionaires because they heard me shouting and having fun on an audio app, to speaking and training big multinationals because they connected with my unique style. This is what I want for you. I want you to find your own way of thinking, feeling and doing to expand your global impact.

In this chapter, I will explore the idea of adopted authenticity and how it influences your personal life and career. Then, we'll dive into strategies to help you break free from the ordinary and embrace your true self, using an ice cream parlour as an example. Lastly, we'll discover and nurture your compelling attractiveness to maximise your impact as a leader.

Adopted authenticity

I was born in Caracas and, at the age of five, moved with my family to a smaller town by the sea in the east of the country. I didn't look too different from the people there, but definitely sounded miles apart. This made me stand out, which led to kids making fun of me. This was the first time I can recall feeling ashamed of myself.

I didn't like the feeling, so what did I do? I tried to change to fit in. But I would then go back to Caracas for a holiday, and would have to re-adopt the accent and style to be accepted there. Tiring, yes, but I didn't know to do any different. And this is how I spent the majority of my childhood and adolescence.

As I shared previously, at sixteen I moved to Sweden, where I was a complete alien. I didn't have much of an accent because my English was limited and my Swedish non-existent, but I had to adapt to their rules and culture. I was quite extroverted and had to tone it down because the Swedes were quiet at school, something I wasn't much used to. Again, I tried to fit in and adopted many of their values and behaviours – and had one of the best years of my life.

I went back to Venezuela and, somehow, I started feeling more comfortable in my own skin. Whether I was in Cumana, Caracas or any other city, I would stick to my own accent and style. I started feeling different in a good way, and standing out wasn't as bad as before. I think living abroad gave me a sense of confidence in what I was capable of, after all I had learned two languages and managed to live in a completely different country.

At the age of twenty-four I left Venezuela for good, searching for a new life in Spain. I went back to my five-year-old self. I struggled with my accent because people were constantly asking me where I was from, and many called me 'the Venezuelan' instead of Jose. I felt attacked (though I'm not saying that was people's intention).

Yet again, a conundrum. What to do? Even though I had some great experiences, both professionally and personally, I never fully adapted and, again, I always felt like an alien. A year later, I was headed to the UK. Initially, a lot of people said to me, 'You need to take diction lessons. You sound too foreign, people won't take you seriously,' and so on and so forth.

Up to this point, my life had pretty much always felt like a battle between who I am and who others thought I should be – and the others were winning almost every time. By always adapting to the situations and adopting the established ways, I was never fully happy with who I was, never challenging people and never stepping up for myself.

Even though your story will be different to mine, you will have your own version of adopted authenticity from which you communicate. In the process, you experience fear, uncertainty, insecurity and a lack of confidence. You want to do the right thing and not upset people. You start paying too much attention to what others might think or say about you. You feel your accent is too strong, imposter syndrome kicks in and you believe people will think less of you because of your origins. The list goes on.

If you continue to communicate from this place of adopted authenticity, you will influence people, because we always do. But will you influence them to the best of your potential, to help them achieve theirs? Do you want your adopted authenticity to be passed onto the people you lead? I hope your answer is, 'No way, Jose. That's not what I want.' Otherwise, you are in trouble.

You might ask, 'Jose, don't we all have a level of adopted authenticity? If we are a result of the influence of our parents, friends, teachers, culture, experiences?' And yes, you'd be right.

My goal is for you to recognise who you are, start peeling layers to unveil your essence, your most congruent self where you feel at ease with who you are and have clarity on what you want. This will change and evolve, and so will you, but you'll do this by being proactive instead of reactive.

Not everyone will like you – but not everyone likes you now. The point is, by being *you*, the impact you can have will be greater. It will set you apart in your own right and will attract incredible opportunities, experiences and people to your life, career and business. Consciously or unconsciously, people will want what you have: the freedom to be themselves.

When you don't proactively work on your authenticity, you are not paying enough attention to either your strengths or limitations, to the beliefs and values that lead your actions; to the things that make you unique; to the things that make you who you are. Developing your authenticity as a leader with global influence will enable you to be comfortable in uncomfortable situations, and to have difficult conversations without fear of saying the wrong thing because it may upset somebody. At the same time, you will have no problem being vulnerable, admitting a mistake or apologising. You will continuously stretch yourself and, in the process, will influence others to stretch themselves too and be more at ease in their own skin. You will gain a unique degree of compelling attractiveness by being open and easy to deal with, as well as trustworthy and believable.

Remember that failing is part of this process, and all failure represents is feedback – opportunities to improve and move forward. Without failure there is no progress. So if you are making mistakes, this means you are trying new things and implementing some of the ideas in this book. My advice? Dare to fail, learn quickly and get on with it.

 Experience the freedom of being you and dare to fail more often.

Next, I will introduce you to my 'be less vanilla' philosophy, which I developed specifically to add value to your authenticity discovery process.

Be less vanilla, be more you

When you hear the word 'vanilla', you may or may not think about ice cream. You may also wonder, what does this have to do with global influence or authenticity? Let me explain.

After looking on Google Trends for the most popular ice cream flavours worldwide, guess what I found was number one? Vanilla, closely followed by chocolate. That probably comes as no surprise. Well, let me tell you a surprising story.

Upon my return from Sweden back in 1998, I started collaborating with AFS, the organisation I did my exchange student trip with. For a while I used to take international students around the city I lived in, but one time, we made a trip across the country, starting in Margarita Island in the east and travelling all the way to the Andes in the west, close to the Colombian border. We stopped at various cities to look at the main attractions and most iconic places. This is when I experienced Heladería Coromoto for the first time. It's an ice cream parlour that offers over 800 ice cream flavours. Yes, you read that right.

Heladería Coromoto was founded in the early eighties by Manuel Da Silva Oliveira, a Portuguese immigrant who, like my Spanish grandparents and many others, left his home nation looking for new opportunities and a better life in a new country. Venezuela used to be that country.

The most interesting part is that when Mr Oliveira started Coromoto, they only had four flavours: vanilla, chocolate, strawberry and coconut. You might think that coconut seems quite unique, but that's not the case in Venezuela where this dry drupe is very popular. So far, there isn't much that's special about this parlour. But then they launched their avocado flavour, which became a hit. This was the beginning of a new phase, when they began to experiment with a variety of flavours, ranging from shellfish all the way to black beans, tropical cocktails, national dishes and more. When I visited the place, it was packed, and I wondered why. They dared to try new things, to be less vanilla and more unique, which enabled them to stand out internationally, to the extent that they won a Guinness World Record – no small feat.

This story inspired me to write and speak about the importance of being less vanilla and more authentic and unique instead. There is enough vanilla in this world, so I invite you to discover your own flavour, your unique way of doing things and impacting people as an international leader.

This is how I see it. Imagine your adopted authenticity as a bowl with three vanilla ice cream scoops; as you become less vanilla and more authentic, you begin to replace the vanilla scoops with your own flavour, whatever that might be. How can you translate this metaphor and use it to increase your ability to positively lead and influence your people? There are three things you can do:

1. Work on your unique and unreasonable dreamscape

2. Dare to fail

3. Stay hungry

Let's explore each of these in more detail.

Work on your unique and unreasonable dreamscape

This is all about gaining clarity regarding what you want to achieve as an international leader, the impact you wish to create and how you want to be perceived.

This is where you paint your vision on the canvas of your mind.

Here is an example of a unique and unreasonable dreamscape. You have been appointed as the manager that will lead the future growth of a division of the business internationally. Now, answer the following question: where do you want the business to be in one, two and three years? If the answer doesn't scare you, it means it's reasonable. If the path to get there seems achievable, it's not challenging enough – it's vanilla and not so unique.

Usually, the scariest dreamscape is the one that will deliver the greatest value to you and the people you lead. Think of it as your version of the avocado flavour launch.

Dare to fail

In many cultures, failure is still not perceived as a good thing. At school and through most of our student careers, we are penalised with poor grades when we make mistakes. I still remember being hit by my teacher with a wooden ruler in front of the whole classroom because I didn't know the answer to a maths problem. I was only eight – no wonder I still doubt myself when it comes to maths. There is a possibility for a mistake? No, thank you – I would rather do nothing than the wrong thing.

As Daniel Pink writes in *Drive: The surprising truth about what motivates us,* during the Industrial Revolution, the carrot-and-stick style of motivation was normalised as the way to reward positive behaviour and results, and to punish the opposite. When you did the right thing and followed the rules, you would get the carrot. And when you didn't, or made mistakes in the process, the much-desired reward would be withheld. No room for experimentation was allowed. This is a creativity and initiative killer.

A different approach to this, and a great way to influence people's motivation, is by giving them autonomy and permission to fail. To do this, you need to give yourself permission to fail too. Make sure that this failure happens within the parameters of your unique and unreasonable dreamscape.

If your new ice cream flavour launch fails, collect feedback, implement the necessary changes and relaunch – or maybe change the flavour? The speed at which you deal with failure and move on will be one of your many authenticity traits.

Stay hungry

Not so that you can eat lots of ice cream, but so that you remain consistent in your actions to achieve your dreamscape, even when it changes – which generally it does. The 'be less vanilla, be more authentic' road can be tiring, tricky and challenging at times, because it requires you to always be flexible and adaptable in order to learn what you need to improve and get to the next level in whatever you do. It's the opposite to complacency, so staying hungry – especially when it comes to dealing with adversity and the unexpected obstacles that will emerge along the way – will help you stay on track.

Be more authentic

Decide on your own stretch, not what anybody else thinks it should be. The healthiest competition is the one you have with yourself. This is how I want you to think about your authenticity. It's a self-discovery process whereby you will gain awareness of your weaknesses and turn them into strengths, while also leveraging your existing strengths. The real beauty comes from accepting your limitations and learning how to turn them into assets.

There are a variety of elements that are part of what makes us authentic but if I can condense the essence of it for you to work on something more tangible, the two I consider the most important are self-confidence and competence.

Cultivate your self-confidence

The whole process starts within. To be less vanilla and be more authentic is a mindset, a muscle that can only be strengthened if you exercise it. It's like going to the gym, running or doing martial arts. It can be challenging at the beginning, but it will improve with time and practice. Your understanding of what you stand for, who you are, what you believe about yourself and what you value, is the foundation for the behaviours you show in your interactions with people and events.

To assess your current self-confidence, there are some questions you can answer. First, think of something you would like to achieve, a goal:

- From a scale of one to ten, how much do you believe in your ability to achieve that goal?

- What gives you confidence that you will achieve it? These are things you should do/think more.

- What takes away your confidence that you will achieve it? These are things you should do/ think less.

We tend to be quick to admit our lack of confidence, but how often do we proactively work to develop it? Confidence can be contextual; you will find that there are circumstances where you feel more confident than others. Answering the above questions will help you focus on an area you want to work on or goal you want to reach, and identify the things you can do/think more or less to build up your self-confidence.

Grow your competence

Confidence grows with increased competence, so focus on developing and mastering your skills.

A good question for you right now is: where do you need to increase your competence in order to achieve your desired goal? Link this to the goal from the self-confidence exercise above. There might be more than one area where you need to become more competent.

As you begin to grow more confident and comfortable in your own skin, because not only do you believe more in yourself, but you also continuously invest in your competence, start thinking about what you want your compelling attractiveness to be. Think of this as your unique mix.

The 'be less vanilla, be more authentic' philosophy is aimed at helping you discover, recognise and expand on what makes you unique within the international communication and influence business context, which is what I define as your *compelling attractiveness*. This is about finding the right balance between your ability to be open, receptive and supportive while also being critical, direct and trustworthy. This is what will make people trust you and respect you.

How attractive and how compelling are you?

You may not have thought about this question until this point – well, it's time. In an international leadership context, attractiveness has to do with you being approachable, inviting, easy to talk to, fresh and original. If people like you, they will feel attracted to you.

In the same context, being compelling is related to how credible and knowledgeable you are, whether you evoke interest, admiration and inspiration through your conviction. If people respect you, they will listen to you.

Think about it this way, attractiveness opens the door and being compelling will seal the deal. You need to be both to be an influential global leader.

When I decided to support business leaders to communicate with impact and confidence, it was because my self-confidence and competence had reached a level at which I knew I could provide high value to my clients. This was achieved through time, experience and results. The same applies to you. As you increase your confidence and competence, you will begin to stand out and will be perceived in a certain way within your business. You need confidence to become more authentic and will need to work on your compelling attractiveness to consciously influence how people perceive you. There will be situations where you will need to dial up your attractiveness and dial down how compelling you are, and vice versa. The best way to find out how you are being perceived is to ask your team members for feedback. It's that simple.

As I've mentioned a few times, human interactions are always unique and, as a leader with global influence, your mission is to get people to act even when they lack confidence, are fearful or feel uncomfortable. This is probably your greatest gift because you will be getting them out of their comfort zone, where there is space for growth and expansion. To do this, you will need a huge level of flexibility and adaptability to be able to communicate in a way that compels them to act. You will have to figure out what the right balance is for each interaction based on the person, the situation and the intended results you have in mind.

CASE STORY - 'JOSE, I'VE PUT MY NOTICE IN!'

I didn't see this one coming and I have to say, it was a pleasant surprise. Ross, International Head of Operations at a multinational logistics company, attended one of my leadership and communication sessions and, throughout our time together, he showed high emotional intelligence and extreme care and concern for people - very important qualities of a Global Influence Leader.

I spoke about topics ranging from the role of a leader, the importance of a clear vision, mission and values within the business and, most importantly, the teams we lead, all the way to feedback, coaching and conflict management.

Ross was pensive during the session and, a few weeks later, I received news from him and, I quote: 'Jose, you confirmed a lot of what was in my mind over those two days. It wouldn't have happened without hearing your views and seeing how much you believed in yourself.'

This was after he had shared his decision to move to a company where people are appreciated and that has clear values. He'd received two job offers within the first two weeks after our session and took the one that resonated with him the most along with a substantial salary increase.

Seeing how much I believed in myself had had an impact on Ross. Adopted authenticity wouldn't have had the same level of influence, proving that being more you, sticking to your values and beliefs and speaking with passion about what you love, will have positive repercussions on others that are beyond the imaginable. This is what I want for you.

 Remember, there is enough vanilla out there. Be more authentic, be more you, believe in yourself and start creating your own global influence.

Self-reflection

- What aspects of your past have influenced your tendency to adopt different personas or behaviours to fit in or be accepted? How have these adaptations shaped your sense of self and affected your confidence and authenticity?

- Have there been instances in your life when you felt a strong sense of authenticity and confidence? How can you replicate or enhance those conditions in your current life and career?

- Consider a recent challenge or opportunity where you chose to step into your authentic self and express your unique style. How did you feel during and after that experience? What positive outcomes or reactions did you observe from others, and how did this impact your confidence and influence?

- In the pursuit of becoming a more authentic and influential leader, what specific actions can you take to keep cultivating both your self-confidence and competence?

Action points

- Unveil your unique authenticity. Begin a self-discovery journey to uncover your genuine essence, values and strengths – these are what make you unique.

- Define ambitious goals that align with your authentic self, ones that may initially seem challenging or even intimidating.

- Imagine your ideal future as a global leader and envision the impact you want to create on an international scale.

- Actively work on developing self-confidence by focusing on the areas that contribute to your talents and achievements.

- Assess how attractive (your approachability, openness) and compelling (your credibility, knowledge) you currently are. Aim to strike a balance between the two to expand the reach of your influence.

FIVE
Internationality

I know, 'internationality' is not a word. Well it is now. And it's not just about international awareness, which focuses on the ability to understand, respect and work well with people from diverse cultures. Internationality is the heart of international human interactions, and its aim is to increase connectivity amongst people. For greater influence, you need deeper bonds.

In this chapter, I will explain the concept of internationality, starting with viewing alienation through a different lens, and then talking about the levels of energy we bring into our human interactions. I will conclude by drawing upon some family wisdom.

Let's get stuck in.

The alienation game

I'm excited to dive into this topic, which can generate a good amount of controversy nowadays. I don't want more controversy; I'm only after solutions and new approaches to deal with our cross-cultural communication challenges.

My first week in the UK, I was asked to mind the phones at the business I had started working in. I thought my English was up to the challenge and so did my manager. I realised that wasn't the case when I answered the first call to a person dialling in from Dundee, a city in the north of Scotland. After a few attempts of me trying to understand the woman on the phone, while apologising about the fact that I couldn't make sense of what she was asking for, she hung up on me – but not before shouting, 'You are useless!'

I experienced similar scenarios through-out the day. The outcome was a huge blow to my confidence. Experiences can make or break you. Being new in the country, it certainly broke me for a while. On top of that, this person, who was a regular cus-  tomer, kept phoning the office and referring to me as Mohamad, which, clearly, isn't my name. How's that for being alienated?

I didn't see it back then, but alienation can be seen as a game. At the time, I could never have conceived it this way, but as the years have gone by, I've come to terms with it. Seeing it as a game also takes a lot of the negativity and other emotions out of the equation.

What do I mean by a game? I'm a human being, so are you and so is the lady from Dundee. When she said I was useless and called me by the wrong name, I felt like an undesired immigrant, a complete alien who had no business in the UK. I don't think she knew the impact her words would have on me, but for a while she became my tormentor.

The above scenario is obviously not okay and was insensitive on the part of the caller, but what I've been sensing more and more is the opposite situation: we non-native speakers, immigrants or direct descendants of them, are growing oversensitive in how we expect people to communicate with us. It's great to raise standards but we must also remain flexible, because otherwise we might be building up barriers that restrain others from openly engaging with us. This will reduce our attractiveness and, therefore, our influence within the international playground.

This message is also for native speakers, encouraging them to be more empathetic and internationally aware when engaging with people from other cultures. For additional information on this, you can refer back to the SIMPLER framework in chapter one.

Changing the game with FOAM

How can we change the game dynamics? Within the context of leading with global influence, being proactive is key. Those who find themselves easily tormented can benefit from focusing on FOAM, instead of adding fuel to the fire:

Flexibility is about how we perceive situations in our life. If we are always being attacked, we become victims. If we change our perception, we can become more resourceful. If I'd applied flexibility to my phone scenario, I would have asked myself questions like:

- Has she been exposed to other cultures and accents in the past?

- What could be going on in her world to make her behave this way?

- What can I learn from this?

This would have put me in a position of strength or, even better, influence. Not necessarily to influence *her*, but it would definitely have changed my state and thinking around the situation.

Taking **ownership** of these scenarios will put the ball in your court. You don't need to condone people's behaviours, but you can orchestrate the process to improve the outcomes. After my phone encounter, I started taking lessons to not only improve my English but to learn the industry's terminology. Always take charge.

At the same time, the tormentor could do with increased adaptability. **Adaptability** means you communicate with the person you have in front of you, on the phone or on the other side of a screen, not who you think they are. Be curious and adapt your style and language to benefit the other person. Had I reacted aggressively towards the person on the phone, I would have potentially turned into her tormentor. In this hypothetical situation, she could have been more resourceful by elevating her flexibility, ownership and adaptability. Otherwise, the tormentor–tormented cycle would have continued.

For those of you who are not familiar with the expression, '**mind the gap**' is a warning phrase used on the London Underground, alerting passengers to be careful when boarding the carriage because there is usually a gap between the train and the platform edge.

The same warning applies to our human interactions. The gap is the differences that exist between us in terms of our realities, culture and language. Our goal as international communicators is to close that gap.

In the process, we will make mistakes, we will say the wrong thing on more than one occasion, but if we consistently adapt and continue to find new ways to bridge the gap and bring us closer and connect, we are on the right path towards growing our influence. Remember that your words can help build people's sculptures or chisel them away. We are all responsible for the words we use and also for how we respond to the words that others use to communicate with us.

Do you see now how the game works? And can you begin to play it differently? When communicating, adapt your message to the other person and, when on the receiving end, be flexible in your interpretation, own your response and adapt it to the other party. This can become a healthy cycle.

I hope this chapter also serves as inspiration for people to change their ways, to be more open and accepting of mistakes; to be less reactive and defensive; to go the extra mile to understand people's intentions; to be empathetic, compassionate, patient and respectful of others. There is no need for more aggression; what we need is to change our perceptions to improve our comprehension.

Think proactively about how to deal effectively with these scenarios if you ever come across them. Break the tormentor–tormented cycle and put out the fire with FOAM.

The energy intensity in human interactions

Energy intensity is the amount of energy used to produce a given level of output or activity. In our context, we will define it as the amount of energy shown in our behaviours as a result of our communication.

According to National Geographic, there are seven continents in the world and the UN recognises 193 countries. Depending on the source you consult, there are more than 3,000 cultures and 7,000-plus languages (IsAccurate, 2021; Lingua, 2022). These figures may vary slightly, but they're significant. I had to come up with a way to simplify my advice for international communication, otherwise this book wouldn't be practical. So I've come up with some ground rules based on energy intensity to help us all navigate the international waters of human interactions.

It all started back in 1998. (I know, here I go again with another story.) In August, I found myself in Sweden, in a small city near Stockholm, surrounded by people from all around the world – I kid you not, almost every nationality was present at this gathering, a weekend camp for students to meet and receive an induction regarding the year ahead. That weekend, I experienced a combination of excitement, curiosity and admiration all at the same time, which led me to speak with every person I came across. All this with limited English.

In the evening, the hosts put together a small party for the students to have some fun. This is where my human energy theory was born. People were dancing and chatting, and the distribution of the room caught my attention. Towards the centre, I predominantly found Latin Americans surrounded by the Spanish, Portuguese, Italians, Greeks, Turks, Nigerians and Ghanaians. As the circle opened up, I could see Americans, people from Balkan countries, England, India, Canada, Australia, Belgium, the Netherlands, Germany, Austria, Czech Republic, Latvia, Sweden, Russia, China, Japan, Korea, Singapore and Thailand. I'm sure I'm missing some countries, but I have enough samples to support what's coming next.

I noticed different levels of energy in the room. Towards the centre, it was hot, maybe because more people were dancing, but the intensity was high. As you moved out of the circle, it would get either more relaxed (medium intensity) or colder (low intensity). This is not when understanding dawned on me (it took me years to fully make sense of this theory), but that party was the first piece of the puzzle.

Almost a decade later, I found myself at an international show, celebrating, again with many nationalities under one roof. I experienced a similar feeling to what I had in Sweden. (This was before inhibitions went out the window because of the drinks and music.) People were beginning to sit at their tables, and I could easily tell the hot tables from the cold and the more relaxed ones. I could predict what would happen next. Again, the hot tables were the first to go towards the dance floor in the middle and, as the night continued, a similar scenario unfolded to what had happened at my exchange student party ten years previously. The colder and more relaxed energies started to gather around and, in the end, we all became one big circle of international people dancing, connecting and having fun.

This confirmed my theory – the first time I had experienced this, I was still a boy surrounded by young students, but the second time I was in an international business setting with people of different ages, career backgrounds and industries. What I'd noticed in Sweden wasn't just because we were young, it had something to do with cultures and, of course, individual personalities.

The next day, as I walked through the exhibition, the same thing happened again. Entering the halls where Asian companies were based, I would experience an air of calmness and comfort; with the northern and eastern Europeans, it was a little cold and reserved at first; for the southern Europeans, Americans and Latin Americans, it was warmer and more welcoming. Regardless of this, I was still able to connect with many of them and have great conversations once I managed to break through that initial energy, which had different levels of intensity. It felt almost like a bubble that, once burst, would allow the human being within to appear.

For the high-intensity people, the initial conversation would happen fairly easily and would flow naturally, but was generally led by them. The calmer and more balanced (medium intensity) people would also have this invisible separation, which generally took the form of a respectful silence. On these occasions, I would tend to lead the conversation. Finally, for the colder temperature people (lower intensity), it was like there was an invisible barrier that disappeared once they warmed up to me. Initially, it felt like distrust, but after the two-way conversation began this would vanish.

At this point, I thought I had a valid theory, but I needed more field experimentation. I continued with my international business travels, having meetings with clients, suppliers and business colleagues, eating breakfast, lunch and dinner together, meeting their families. These interactions enabled me to corroborate what I had already realised in terms of the energy intensity, but there was much more still to unveil.

When the initial bubble was burst, this represented an opportunity to connect with the person, a unique human being with beliefs, values, strengths, weaknesses and fears. Can you see where this is going? What's inside the bubble tends to look quite similar, regardless of countries and cultures. More on this later.

As I continued with my international human interactions, I began to recognise that there were elements that stood out at the initial contact. For the people with high energy intensity, the element that would stand out to me at first would be ego. There was a level of self-importance that would come through. The people with a calm and more relaxed energy (medium intensity) had a softer and comfortable demeanour. Here it all seemed to be about respect; embracing this mutual respect and admiration would help them to open up. Lastly, with the cold or lower-intensity people, when I think of them the word 'trust' stands out. It was all about enticing them. Finding a way to break the ice (pun intended).

An important note: the above are generalisations based on my years of international business travels and also of coaching, training and speaking. I generalise in order to simplify a subject that tends to create complications. Human beings are complex creatures, and my frameworks and theories are intended to provide you with a helpful starting point when engaging with people across cultures. Use them with flexibility and adapt them to each scenario.

No one energy, temperature, colour or word will ever define a person, because there are no absolutes. We are a spectrum and we are always changing.

Keep this in mind as you continue to develop your global influence. This is your challenge – it's no small feat.

Increasing your internationality

Internationality, within the context of this book, means that you operate in more than one country and that you possess the ability to create deep and long-lasting connections with people, regardless of their cultural background and/or country of origin. Remember that although this is a business book, what you learn here can also be applied to other areas of your life.

Think of internationality as the heart of international human connections. As a leader who is developing their global influence, internationality lies at the centre of everything. Take internationality as a verb, not a noun. Exercise it.

The Latin proverb that all roads lead to Rome doesn't apply here because the way in which you connect with people will be unique to you, just like the influence you will have and the impact it will create. So what's your unique recipe?

I'm going to share mine with you. I call it my grandad strategy. Consider everything you've learned from reading the book this far and add to that: excitement, admiration, humour and humility. This will increase your connectivity. Allow me to explain.

Maria Franzoni, who kindly agreed to write the foreword for this book and who's been coaching me to revamp my speaking business positioning, once asked me, 'Jose, how do you connect with people?' My mind took me straightaway to my grandad and then to feeling excitement. All very emotional and very me. Remember the heart, mind, body core areas from chapter two? The heart is the place I recommend starting your communication from.

Let me tell you about my grandad. Apart from my *abuela* (grandma), I never heard anyone say anything negative about him. What I did hear a lot of was people laughing around him, asking him for help, support and advice, giving him praise. At work, people loved him and had only positive things to say about him. I see him as a good role model for a leader with international influence. But how did he do it? How did he get people to want to be around him, to trust and respect him? He had one hell of a unique compelling attractiveness.

Based on my memories of him, everything that he taught me and how he guided me, combined with how I've managed to connect and positively influence people from all walks of life, this is what I came up with. This, I think, was the key to his success and, to an extent, to mine.

As I mentioned above, it's about injecting excitement, admiration, humour and humility to your human interactions. But I spiced them up a notch. To increase your internationality, you need:

- **Adjustable excitement:** According to the Oxford Languages Dictionary, excitement is a feeling of great enthusiasm and eagerness. Wouldn't you like people to be eager to meet you, to talk to you? It's difficult to say no to this. Too much excitement can put people off but what I'm talking about here is just the right amount (hence, adjustable). Be excited, but regulate it based on the person you are engaging with.

- **Channelled admiration:** Admiring others is positive because it means you are curious and are paying attention to the person and, in return, they can feel appreciated. Admiration is also connected to respect and a sense of approval. The 'channelling' aspect here means it's directed at something in particular, like a behaviour, strength, an activity they perform well, an element of their culture, etc. Proactively look for areas to channel your admiration towards.

- **Purposeful humour:** This is not about cracking jokes to make people laugh but more about a mood and a state of mind. The ability to be amused by things will take the edge off on how you perceive them and will likely bring a feeling of lightness to your communication and relationships. When you are often amused you don't take things too seriously, which can give you additional flexibility and resources when dealing with people and especially challenging scenarios. Be purposeful with your humour and please, don't use it to deflect difficult or uncomfortable conversations or situations.

- **Determined humility:** In your role as a leader with global influence, whatever you do is intended to create an impact on people, so it's not about you – they are the ones who matter. Being modest, putting any pride and arrogance aside will ground you and make you more human. You won't waste energy feeding your ego and thinking you are better or worse than others. You are not in competition; you are collaborating with and supporting your people. Be determined to remain humble, it's a powerful trait.

Master the above, be excited but adjust the feeling depending on the person and situation, channel your admiration for them, be often amused and use your humour with purpose while remaining humble, and you will increase your influence and ability to connect. These traits can be perceived as weaknesses by some people, but they can become your greatest strengths when building deeper, authentic and long-lasting connections across cultures and, more importantly, among humans.

My *abuelo* (grandad) loved connecting with people. Now you have a breakdown of his strategy, revamped with my experience and insights from having implemented it myself over the years. Apply it and carry on increasing your internationality.

CASE STORY – 'JOSE, I CAN'T MOTIVATE MY TEAM ANYMORE!'

Alice is the manager of an international team that she leads remotely due to the members' worldwide locations. Recently she has been somewhat frustrated because the team is not achieving the results she expects, and she senses that their motivation has dropped.

During a coaching session, we had the following conversation:

ME: Alice, has anything changed in terms of how you interact with your team?

ALICE: I'm not sure. I've been under a lot of stress and so has the team. I may have been dropping the ball with them as well.

At this point, my intuition suggested that I take her through my *abuelo*'s framework, because I was sensing a lack of connection between her and the team under the current circumstances. Based on this, my next question was:

ME: How excited have you been lately about work and projects overall?

ALICE: Not very, Jose.

ME: In terms of admiration, have you been proactive in your praises?

ALICE: Hmm, not really. It's just been very stressful lately.

ME: I guess there hasn't been much humour either?

(A leading question, based on previous answers.)

ALICE: It hasn't been fun lately.

ME: Have you been humble and vulnerable with them?

ALICE: What do you mean?

ME: Have you shared your frustrations and the mistakes you've made? You mentioned having dropped the ball.

This led to further realisations on her part and prompted clear actions and behavioural changes. For example, she chose to be more proactive in praising her team, openly sharing some of her frustrations and bringing a more optimistic outlook to her interactions with them.

This is not the only valid approach here; however, this framework can help you, amongst other things, to recognise your energy levels and state of being when interacting with your team.

 Your team will feed off the energy you convey through your leadership.

Self-reflection

- How do you currently handle cross-cultural communication challenges, and what are some instances where you felt alienated or misunderstood in an international context?

- Are you oversensitive in how you expect others to communicate with you in cross-cultural interactions? How can you balance raising standards while remaining flexible to build deeper connections?

- Reflecting on the concept of energy intensity, what patterns have you noticed in your cross-cultural interactions regarding initial energy levels? How can you adapt your approach based on the energy intensity of the people you engage with?

- What steps can you take to foster deeper and more authentic connections internationally?

Action points

- Apply the FOAM model: be flexible in your perception of situations, take ownership of your responses, adapt your communication style and mind the gap that exists between different cultures and perspectives.

- Recognise that different cultures and individuals bring varying levels of energy to their interactions.

- Embrace the 'bubble' idea, where initial energy levels might differ, but as connections deepen, common human qualities emerge.

- Find the right level of excitement, adjusted to the person and situation. Channel admiration towards specific aspects of others to show genuine interest and respect. Develop purposeful humour to create a lighter atmosphere and maintain flexibility. Practise determined humility to ground yourself, collaborate and build stronger connections.

- Exercise your internationality by creating deep connections across cultures and countries. Embrace your unique approach to connecting with people, focusing on their needs and fostering long-lasting relationships.

SIX

The Channels Of Global Influence

Recently, while speaking to a group of young leaders at a London event, I asked about their upbringing, specifically whether their parents had asked many questions or simply told them what to do. Except for one person, everyone reported the latter. This pattern of telling and directing generally continues in the workplace, as bosses and managers often replicate the same approach. However, there is an alternative, a more effective approach based on the concepts of push and pull and the 3Cs of global influence.

Push, pull and the 3Cs

The 'telling' situation I described above is known as a 'push' in communication, influence and even

marketing. When we do this, we are pushing information, our understanding of reality, experiences,
knowledge, insights, instructions, feedback onto the
people we lead. Too much of this approach and we
are not empowering our people but building robots
instead. Don't get me wrong, there is a place for pushing and it's important, but it's just as important to do
the opposite, known as 'pull'.

When we pull, we ask more questions; we listen to
understand; we reflect, paraphrase and summarise
to enable the other person to develop their initiative, become more autonomous and self-reliant, grow
their confidence, competence and intrinsic motivation.
Powerful, isn't it? Now imagine the results you can
achieve by using the two approaches more intentionally and in a balanced way, adapted to the person's
needs at a specific moment.

When it comes to communication, there are three
effective strategies that can help you influence people
and create a positive shift in their perspectives and
actions. These strategies involve adopting certain personas, which I refer to as the '3Cs':

1. **The conveyor:** this involves directing and telling
   people what to do, providing clear instructions
   and guidance to achieve desired outcomes.

2. **The coach:** this approach revolves around asking
   individuals how they would handle a situation,

encouraging their input and guiding them towards their own solutions.

3. **The challenger:** by challenging the way people are currently approaching things and fostering healthy discussions, you can stimulate critical thinking, creativity and innovation, leading to positive changes in their behaviours and commitment levels.

Let's dive into these in a bit more depth.

The conveyor: 'Let me tell you...'

This strategy focuses on delivering information in a manner that prompts individuals to shift and act. When presenting information within this framework, frankness will be crucial, but your approach should be tailored to the individual, cultural context and situation. This is laying the groundwork for effective ongoing communication, and you may need to acquaint the person with this style if it diverges from their typical approach. Things like the SIMPLER, FOAM and TACO models can be used to enhance your adaptability, trust and understanding while conveying information in multicultural environments. Here I'm only referring to one-to-one communication. In chapter nine I explain how to communicate with impact in front of an audience, which is also a key skill for your global influence toolbox.

When taking on the role of the conveyor, the goal is to communicate from a point that integrates heart, mind and body. This will enable you to feel what you want to say and to think about the person you are saying it to; to rationalise the situation to find the best way to say something so that it has the intended impact; and to present the message with congruence in your physiology and tonality. These skills represent the basis for the conveyor.

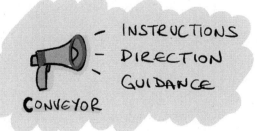

In this section, I want to specifically delve deeper into the role of the conveyor in providing feedback to team members because, when used and embraced purposely, it can be an effective strategy to positively impact people's behaviours.

Time and time again I hear from businesses that want to incentivise a feedback culture within the organisation because they understand the benefits that can be obtained when we take the time to share what we think about something, and when the person on the receiving end can learn and grow from the experience. Who doesn't want that? But there are some potential challenges. The main one is when feedback is not one of the values of the organisation, nor a common practice within your team. Another challenge is faced where people are not properly trained to give feedback. They may have frameworks but they don't apply them because they are afraid of upsetting the other person or being disliked as a result. Can you relate?

The angle I'd like you to consider is that feedback is never about the person but their behaviour, and its effectiveness will depend on how it is delivered and how it is received. It requires flexibility from both sides.

A simple structure you can use to craft your feedback is:

1. Highlight the behaviour

2. Convey the impact the behaviour is having

3. Offer a suggestion or ask for theirs

Let's use an example. You have a colleague, her name is Carmen, and she is always on the phone during meetings, which creates disruptions. In giving her feedback on this, following the above structure, you could say something like:

- **Behaviour:** 'Hi, Carmen, I've noticed you are on the phone during our meetings.'

- **Impact:** 'This is creating disruptions and the meetings are taking longer than they need to because I need to repeat the information.'

- **Suggestion:** 'Would you please not use the phone during meetings.' Or, 'What could you do differently in order to avoid using the phone during our meetings?'

In three simple steps you can go straight to the point, highlight the behaviour and offer an alternative action. It's not personal; it's just that the person is acting in a way that is not serving the current environment.

The most common responses tend to be acceptance, justification or rejection. Which in our example might be along the lines of:

- **Acceptance:** 'Yes, I will stop using the phone during meetings.'

- **Justification:** 'I need to use the phone because this and that…'

- **Rejection:** 'I don't agree and I'm not the only one using the phone during meetings…'

Prepare for all scenarios and be ready to support the process with coaching questions and conflict management strategies, which I will cover next in this chapter.

The above is an example of constructive feedback, which is what we need to grow and develop. However, you should balance it out with motivational/encouraging feedback every now and then. Following the same three-step structure, let your people know how well they are performing.

Master your feedback technique, make it a crucial value within your team dynamics and let the magic unfold. Some final recommendations for greater impact when delivering feedback are to always:

- Time it well

- Address one behaviour at a time

- Make it specific and actionable

- Seek a positive change

Be clear, concise and consistent in your communication and always tailor your approach to the person you are interacting with.

 Your role as the conveyor is not just about giving orders but about creating a pathway for success through effective communication and direction.

The coach: 'Can I ask you a question?'

The coach is the biggest 'puller' out of the 3Cs. A good analogy here is the fish and the fishing rod. The conveyor will likely just give you the fish, while the coach will give you a road and help you learn how to fish for yourself. Within organisations, both approaches may work, depending on the circumstances. My recommendation is to mix the three approaches for greater impact.

The job of the coach is to move the person towards a desired outcome through questioning and empathetic listening. Here is another analogy: think of the coach as a hairstylist. They need to know the shape of your head, type of hair, any cowlicks and, of course, what you would like as a result at the end of the appointment. The coach will explore what's inside your head, your thinking patterns and the language you use as a result, and will use all this to help you achieve your goal, shift your behaviour or acquire a new perspective.

As a global influential leader, getting people to make a shift needs to be at the forefront of your mind. My SHIFT coaching model can help you achieve just that. It consists of the following steps:

Seek to understand

Actively looking to understand others will get you into an influential state right away, because you stop thinking about you and what you want to say and instead give all your focus to the other person. But what is it that you are seeking to understand? What do you need to pay attention to?

Let's recreate a scenario you might face. You currently lead a team of ten people; you have clearly defined objectives for the group and for individuals and they are all achieving them – except for one person. What could be happening with this team member? It's time to 'seek to understand'.

You invite the person into your office and you begin to unpack the situation through mainly questions and listening (pulling), rather than telling (pushing). On top of questions and empathetic listening, you pay attention to their language, both verbal and body. What's *not* being said? Seeking to understand remains your state all throughout your engagement with the person. It enables you to stay focused, objective and to avoid unhelpful assumptions. Staying curious will improve the quality of your questions.

Harmonise

Harmonising is about gauging the level of connection you have with the person. This is also known as rapport. When there is a breach in harmony, the person may close up, avoid answering your questions or provide untruthful answers. Since you are still seeking to understand, you look for an agreement between the parties involved. Nothing too formal, a simple question like, 'Is it OK if I ask you some questions?' may suffice. Ease the person into it without being too pushy or inquisitive.

You want to be like a shop assistant who offers support, asks you one question at a time and then let's you be. I was looking for a blazer not long ago and I left the store almost immediately after the salesclerk bombarded me with a load of information about all the blazers they had in the store, while sticking close to me. Since he didn't notice how uncomfortable he was making me, I had to ask him to please give me some room to breathe. I could sense he was seeking to understand what I wanted but his approach wasn't right for me. There was no harmony there.

When you coach, ask for permission, check the level of harmony and give the other person space to come up with their own answers. Don't hijack them. Pause and embrace the power of silence.

Intervene

This is the body of your coaching work. Here is where you ask questions to dive deeper and seek further understanding of the situation from the other person's perspective. Coaching is fluid and further questions are asked based on the responses you receive. Remember, you ask in order to unpack and use that information to help the coaching process. It's all happening simultaneously; you are always seeking to understand, checking for harmony and asking questions.

The intervention process can include various kinds of questions.

Openers:

- What would you like to happen at the end of our time together?

- What has to happen for you to know this has been a worthwhile interaction?

- What do you want to get out of our conversation?

Discovery:

- What's stopping you from achieving what you want?

- What has worked for you in the past?

- Are there any insights you already have that you can draw from?

Development:

- If you could change anything right now, what would you change?

- What can you learn now to reach your current goal?

- What positive things are you doing already? Are there any other positive things you could start doing?

Action:

- What's the most important take-away from this conversation and what are you going to do with it?

- How will you hold yourself accountable?

- How will I know you've done what you say you will? And when will it happen by?

These are just some examples of the questions you can use; come up with your own, keep them open and enjoy the process.

Functioning check

Is the conversation moving towards the desired outcome? Coaching is about closing the gap between the current situation/state and the wanted situation/ state, so it's important that you calibrate how your questions are landing and whether they are helping the person reach the intended destination.

Also, make sure that you are noticing positive shifts in behaviours, thinking, 'aha' moments and break-throughs. These are important cues because they indicate the effectiveness of your coaching. In the same way you are checking your harmony levels, you need to keep checking that what you are doing is having a positive impact. This will help you keep the process on track and to avoid deviations in the conversation. A common situation while coaching is that the person may go off on a tangent; you can help them come back and focus on what's needed for them to reach the expected outcomes.

Is your coaching working towards bridging the gap?

Time for action

We need to wrap up at some point. If the person doesn't do anything after the session, it won't be as impactful as if they did. This is why at the end of the coaching you ask for their commitment and a plan as to how they are going to implement their take-aways. Here you can ask some of the action questions I included in the intervene section. Get people to take action to consolidate their shift.

Coaching is an incredible skill that will enable your employees to empower themselves. If you haven't already, start building a coaching culture within your teams and business. There is no need to wait for appraisals to effectively coach your people.

The challenger: 'Actually, I don't agree'

Through careful observation and research, Dr Gottman and Robert Levenson discovered in the 1970s that the key to a lasting relationship is the ability to maintain a positive outlook even in the face of conflict (Benson, no date). What they did was to ask couples to solve a conflict in their relationship in 15 minutes, then sat back and watched. After reviewing the recordings nine years later, they managed to predict with over 90% accuracy which couples would divorce, and which would stay together.

What came out of their study was a 'magic ratio' of five to one, where for every negative interaction during a disagreement, there must be five (or more) positive interactions if the couple is to remain happy together long term. At first glance, it may seem like an intimidating target, but love can bloom and grow only as long as couples continue to make an effort to improve their communication skills by amplifying their positivity when times get tough.

127

How about that? Positive conflict resolution can lead to happy marriages. In the same way, it can lead to improved business relationships. The key success factor here is how we perceive conflict. It can be seen as something uncomfortable that you desperately try to avoid, or as something uncomfortable that, when mastered, can transform your human interactions for the better.

As Patrick Lencioni's second dysfunction of a team, fear of conflict can create an environment where team members don't openly share their thoughts and opinions, or when they do, it's through back channels. This can create resentment, lack of motivation and disproportionately blow up situations that otherwise could have been resolved by diving into a more direct, honest and open conversation.

Learning to thrive in conflict has positively impacted many of my relationships, both professionally and personally, because if I feel it, I rationalise it and then find the best way to convey it – the essence of being assertive. It's important to add here that you're not just saying something because you want to but because you believe the other person needs to hear it for their own benefit. This is the purpose of the global influence challenger: to seek conflict that will eventually lead to a positive outcome. It's important to note that though this will work well on many occasions, you will also fail on others; when the latter happens, learn from the experience and get on with it.

There are many subtleties when it comes to seeking positive conflict, so, let me break down the principles that I recommend you follow:

- Remain extremely curious, observant and caring while listening carefully.

- Look for clarification when needed to make sure you are on the same page as the other person.

- Acknowledge, respect and challenge points of views and address the problems the other person presents to you. Never ignore them.

- When you start feeling uncomfortable, take emotions out of the equation by repeating to yourself, 'This is not personal. It's normal to have disagreements; I can learn something new. It's OK if I'm not liked, accepted or recognised.'

- Ask yourself, 'What could be a positive outcome of this situation?'

- Look for a resolution, which in the end may not be exactly what you intended, but which will hopefully be the best option for the other person and for the relationship moving forward.

- Be vulnerable, admit mistakes and apologise if the situation requires it. Taking your ego out of the way will help you be more objective.

Overall, remember that it's not about you but about the impact you can have on the other person by challenging their current perception of reality.

When it comes to thriving in the face of conflict, old approaches may suggest that you adopt an aggressive or dominant position, which puts the other party on the back foot, resulting in a win for you and loss for them. The opposite approach would be for you to be submissive or passive, which would result in a win for the other person.

In the realm of global influence, it is crucial to strike a balance where both parties benefit from the exchange. Being assertive while showing genuine care for the other person, ensures a win-win situation. It's essential to express your thoughts effectively by considering the other person's perspective.

Kenneth Thomas and Ralph Kilmann, prominent organisational psychologists known for their work in the field of conflict resolution and management, developed a model that identifies five primary conflict-handling modes: competing, accommodating, compromising, avoiding and collaborating. By adopting the right mode in the right situation, you can navigate conflict more effectively and foster positive outcomes for all involved.

Inspired by their work, here is my interpretation of the five modes:

- **Sticking to your guns:** This is when you are defending your opinion or position. (Competing)

- **Giving away the last slice of pizza:** You accept the other person's point of view or take as a final resolution. (Accommodating)

- **Finding balance on a seesaw:** You look for a halfway, to meet in the middle. (Compromising)

- **Ignoring a leaky roof:** You dodge the situation, withdraw from it or postpone it. (Avoiding)

- **Building a puzzle together:** Here you look for mutual benefit. Both parties get what they are looking for. (Collaborating)

This information is extremely valuable, because by understanding what the other person is doing you will be ahead of the game and can either match their behaviour or change it if you think it will facilitate the process. It's likely that you will find yourself moving between the different modes during a conflict.

In your role as a global influence challenger, you will find there are times where ignoring a leaky roof can be a helpful strategy, as you recognise that timing is a key element when it comes to seeking healthy conflict – not every time is the right time. Follow your gut and experiment. Mix and match the above strategies depending on your desired outcomes, how the conversation flows and always keeping the other person's interests at heart.

CASE STORY – 'JOSE, I WANT TO STAND UP FOR MY IDEAS!'

Laura works in the creative industries, at a London-based company. She is responsible for managing a team of fifteen individuals and is more than happy with their performance. She can easily communicate with them and doesn't have any issues having difficult conversations when required. Great news.

But when it comes to managing upwards, defending her ideas and standing up for herself in front of the board of directors, she finds it very difficult. She is Italian and fears that her accent is too strong and that the board may not take her seriously.

I presented to her the conflict-handling modes shared in this chapter and she realised that she was sticking to her guns a lot with her team but, when it came to the board, she would go straight to giving them her last slice of pizza. The stretch for her was to push back more, so I asked a question:

ME: What's one thing you tend to accommodate most of the time?

LAURA: When I present new initiatives, they always shut them down and I don't share how I feel about their decisions.

ME: There you have it. That's your opportunity to start competing and standing up for yourself. You could begin by sharing how you feel and the impact this is likely to have on your motivation and performance, for example. What do you think?

LAURA: It's scary, but I can start one step at a time.

A while later, I received a message from Laura saying: 'Jose, it worked. I've started expressing some of my emotions and, even though they still shut most of my ideas down, I feel more confident, and I've also learned to embrace my accent because it's part of who I am.' I love it when I receive messages like this.

Face your fears head on and adapt your conflict-handling strategies to help you grow and improve.

Self-reflection

- How often do you balance providing information and asking questions in your communication approach?

- How can you integrate the conveyor, coach and challenger strategies to enhance your influence over the people you lead?

- Are you seeking to understand before offering solutions? How can you improve your empathetic listening and harmony-building skills?

- How can you assertively navigate conflict while maintaining respect and empathy, and how can you flexibly switch between conflict-handling modes based on different situations and goals?

Action points

- Balance the push and pull in your communication.

- Master the 3Cs and you will begin to notice change in yourself and those you lead. The mastering process is an exponential one and it will take time. My recommendation is that you take baby steps. This is a journey that can easily take a lifetime of learning and improving and that's the whole idea, that you are always reaching new heights or depths while taking people along with you.

- Give others the privilege of your time and wisdom by conveying, coaching and challenging them in your own, less vanilla global influence leadership style.

- Encourage a feedback culture within your team by focusing on behaviours rather than the individual, fostering growth and improvement.

- Embrace conflict as an opportunity for positive transformation.

PART THREE
EXERCISING YOUR GLOBAL INFLUENCE

In this final part of the book I want you to continue to put ideas, concepts and frameworks into action. By 'exercising' I mean implementation and practice to make sure you get something tangible out of this read.

When it comes to implementation, I want you to think about how everything that we've covered so far, plus what you are about to learn, will fit together and contribute towards achieving your career and business objectives.

In terms of practice, I want you to engage in activities and behaviours repeatedly in order to improve your knowledge base, skills and performance as a leader. For this, I recommend cultivating discipline and consistency to keep honing your abilities and understanding.

It's time to prepare to apply and amplify your global influence.

SEVEN

Fail To Prepare,
Prepare To Fail

Good preparation equips you with a proactive mindset that gets you ready for potential problems and challenges ahead. Not only that, when you are prepared, you feel more confident in your abilities because you've invested in your competence, which will positively impact your performance and help you to handle unexpected situations more effectively.

On your way to becoming a successful leader with global influence, preparation will provide you with clarity, focus, knowledge, adaptability to navigate changing circumstances and environments, enhanced problem-solving skills, and contingency planning by considering different scenarios before they happen. Foremost, it will help you stay alert so that you're able to seize opportunities.

To assist you in your preparation, I'm going to explain how to improve your international communication intelligence, how to use the Global Influence Leader mantras to help you stay on track and, finally, give you my thoughts on how to develop and cultivate a fear-embracing mindset.

International communication intelligence

Nowadays, it's normal to hear about IQ (intelligence quotient) and EQ (emotional quotient), also known as 'emotional intelligence'. But a term I don't hear enough is CQ (communication quotient).

Clare Munn defined CQ as 'expressive and receptive intelligence', representing the communication bridge between IQ and EQ.

We need a certain type of intelligence to be able to explain our thinking, whether that's based on logic, emotions or both. This is where CQ comes in. In simple terms, it is our ability to communicate effectively with one another. You will develop your communication skills by practising, failing and learning along the way, not by knowing all the theories and frameworks available. Learn as much as you can, but make sure you spend at least twice as much time on implementing it.

As you develop and exercise your CQ, it's essential to grasp the inner workings of the parties engaged in the communication process. It all begins with a thought. Based on what you are perceiving, this thought is an indication that you want to communicate something. It may relate to an emotion, reasoning or a combination of both. You then either speak it or write it. This is how you materialise your thought, which now becomes your message.

This is where it gets interesting. The way the person on the receiving end interprets the message will be influenced by their perception of the situation, leading to a unique rational or emotional response. Their feedback will be a valuable contribution to the process, helping you gauge how effectively you've communicated your thoughts.

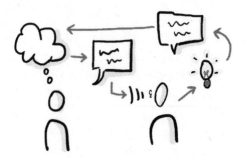

THE COMMUNICATION PROCESS

Simple, right? What could possibly go wrong? Unfortunately, many things. Let me break down some of the challenges that can impact the outcome of your communication:

1. Your perception of the situation might be different from theirs. For example, they see a problem when you see an opportunity.

2. You use words they don't understand, or your message wasn't clear enough.

3. Your tone doesn't meet their expectations.

4. You are too direct or too vague. Too aggressive or too passive.

5. Their feedback doesn't reflect the real effect you have on them. Things are left unsaid.

These are just some of the difficulties you will come across, which is why all the models and frameworks in the world will never replace a hands-on approach.

There are too many variables based on our unpredictable human nature. But hey, it's not all doom and gloom. Below are some ideas on how to deal with the above situations to help you hone your CQ. I call these 'ideas' because there will always be more than one angle. Experiment in your own way.

Situation 1

Your perception of the situation might be different from theirs. For example, they see a problem when you see an opportunity.

Idea: Pay attention to their state and what they say. If you sense stress or frustration, for example, their perception of the scenario may not be the most resourceful. Ask them about their thinking and emotions and explain why you believe it's an opportunity or something positive instead of negative. Ask, listen, unpack and use.

Situation 2

You use words they don't understand, or your message wasn't clear enough.

Idea: Below are some questions to consider that will help you adapt your language and message:

- Who are you communicating with?
- Where are they from?

- What's their English level?

- What's their position within the business?

- How long have they been working with you?

As I shared in chapter one, the first meeting I had when I started working in the UK, I left having understood just 10% of what was thrown at me. Check the person's understanding, ask questions to clarify, be perceptive and avoid being patronising. The SIMPLER framework is helpful in this situation.

Situation 3

Your tone doesn't match their expectations.

Idea: In your head, you are communicating perfectly, but the other person may be perceiving you as shouty, or too slow and quiet. Pay attention to their facial expressions and check in with them. 'Can you hear me OK?' This is especially important in virtual environments when the connection may not be great, which could cause you to break up or sound patchy.

Situation 4

You are too direct or too vague. Too aggressive or too passive.

Idea: Do you know the person you are communicating with? How do they want you to communicate with them? Think about the intensity of your energy and the energy of the person you are engaging with. What can you change? Remember that adaptability is key.

Situation 5

Their feedback doesn't reflect the real effect you have on them. Things are left unsaid.

Idea: Pay attention to body language. You will generally be able to spot changes in the person's face, in their skin (eg flushing) and eye movement. Their tone of voice may also change when there is lack of alignment between their response and how they actually feel.

To really embed this learning, let's consider a real day-to-day scenario. You jump on a Zoom call with Rachel, who is based in Singapore. The reason for the call is to discuss the implementation of a new strategy to get clients. You start by sharing what you think and what you would like her to do. She asks you a few clarifying questions, you answer her questions and at the end she says it's all OK and understood. A week later you jump on a call and find that the strategy hasn't been implemented yet. Why?

What approach would you suggest, based on what you've read so far? Take five minutes to write your ideas down.

International CQ is about having the ability to either avoid the above situation, because you managed to unveil any communication barriers between you and Rachel in the first conversation and dealt with them on the spot. You know this worked because the strategy was implemented successfully. Or, things didn't work out as expected and, as a result, you adapted your approach, found a way to tweak your communication to bridge any cultural barriers and could then positively influence Rachel to implement the strategy beyond your expectations.

CQ involves not only the words spoken but also a focus on how they are being received, ultimately shaping the communication's outcome. Keep in mind that occasional failures in the process are inevitable, but you can assess and use these based on the feedback you receive.

 Always maintain unwavering confidence in the individual's capacity to understand your message and accomplish a task that surpasses your highest expectations.

The Global Influence Leader mantras

I'm a strong believer in having a clear intention and being consistent with your actions to achieve results. This is why I'm presenting these mantras, to help you with your daily preparation process and become more resilient in the face of the many challenges you are likely to encounter as a Global Influence Leader.

The three key benefits of the Global Influence Leader mantras are:

1. **Focus and clarity.** The mantras will provide a focal point for your attention and intention. Think of them as mental anchors that bring clarity and help you stay focused on your vision, mission and values.

2. **Motivation and encouragement.** The mantras consist of positive words and phrases aimed at reinforcing your goals, beliefs and behaviours. This can also boost your confidence and wellbeing, strengthening your ability to bounce back from failure and complete what you set out to achieve.

3. **Self-awareness and self-regulation.** Incorporating these mantras into your daily routine can cultivate heightened self-awareness and regulation. Being present in the moment while observing your thoughts, adjusting your emotions and proactively choosing your responses will be key to positively influencing the people you lead.

The Global Influence Leader mantras are:

- Today I will focus on positively impacting the people I come into contact with.

- I will cultivate the heart, mind and body of my global influence.

- It's important to act, especially when it feels uncomfortable.

- I will actively explore, learn and stretch myself and others.

- The real magic of global influence is the people.

- I'm aware of my adopted authenticity and continuously work to be less vanilla and more me.

- I'm committed to changing how I play the alienation game. The best way to put out the fire is by adding some FOAM.

- We all have different levels of energy when it comes to our human interactions. I understand this is normal and I use it to foster further understanding and appreciation.

- The foundation of internationality is deeply caring for others. It starts with the heart.

- I balance the push and pull in my communication, depending on the situation.

- I'm a conveyor, a coach and a challenger.

- IQ and EQ need CQ for greater impact.

- I proactively face, embrace, act and rethink my fears (next in this chapter).

- I'm aware of the chillies, avocados and ice creams in my environment and adapt my behaviours accordingly. (See chapter eight.)

- I eagerly seek opportunities to address larger audiences, aiming to expand my reach and amplify my message. (See chapter nine.)

- I'm committed to developing and consistently applying my own global influence toolkit.

- By positively impacting the people I lead, I create long-lasting change, organisational growth, and global wealth.

- I'm a leader with global influence.

 Regular practice and wholehearted belief in the power of these mantras can maximise its benefits and results.

Develop a fear-embracing mindset

Fear can be our greatest ally or our worst enemy, it all depends on how we deal with it, process it and understand it. When it comes to fear, I have a confession to make: I always have it, to a greater or lesser degree. Fear is an integral part of me.

In terms of career progression and personal development, embracing fear and using it to your advantage will be incredibly powerful, because on the other side of your fears there is usually something great awaiting you. To me it is not about being fearless but about acting in the presence of fear. Since it's always there, it represents a great fuel and fantastic food for thought.

Why do you think I decided to become a speaker? I love being in front of an audience. I come alive when I'm inspiring, educating, positively influencing and impacting people's lives. Beyond that, I've come to understand that when I stretch myself to achieve new levels of performance, or when I put myself in uncomfortable situations, I'm in charge of my fears and I'm learning from them. Since I always fear something, it means that I'm always learning and improving – as long as I decide to act on it.

To manage fears, you can face them, embrace them, act on them and rethink them.

Face

Proactively acknowledge your fear, whatever it might be. Writing this book has been a challenge for me and even as I'm writing this section, I sense fear disguised as uncertainty as to whether this book will be worth your time. I also fear that some readers may reject it. This is me recognising that fear and doing it anyway.

Embrace

Accept your fear(s) as valid and normal. In the case of writing this book, it's because I'm doing something that I haven't attempted before. By embracing it, I also make the conscious decision to use fear to my own benefit as well as yours. How? If I stop writing, we all lose. So I will continue writing, knowing that if the book is a complete failure, I will find learning and continue forward (this would be the worst case, of course). As I go through this stage, I'm also evaluating and understanding where this fear could be coming from and gauging its intensity. Had I never written articles, trainings and speeches before, I don't think I would have been able to write a book. In this case, fear can highlight that it may not be the right time for you to do something.

Act

When you face and embrace your fear, the next question is what to do with it, or what to do in the situation that is triggering your fear. I always recommend taking some kind of action. Acting with fear is a path to exponential growth, bearing in mind that it doesn't mean jumping off a cliff. This is why the embracing and evaluating stage is important.

If the fear is intense, it may stop you from acting. Here, my suggestion is that you continue taking small steps towards your goal. For example, imagine you want to start applying the global influence challenger approach, but you're uncomfortable about it because it doesn't feel like you. Don't take on the whole thing all at once; you can begin by developing your listening skills, focusing more on the other person. Think about how challenging their views could help them shift and improve. Think about how you would frame it and then, when you are ready, delve into a light conflict, which may be as minor as disagreeing about the quality of the coffee in the office. Practice is key, so take action and keep on stretching.

Rethink

Always take time to rethink your actions. Consider how they went, what could be done differently next time and what you have learned from the experience. Focus on increasing your global influence by saying 'yes' in the face of fear, and taking action, even when it feels uncomfortable.

You can do this right after the action or at the end of your day. The key thing is to set aside dedicated time for thoughtful consideration and to recognise the importance of stepping outside your comfort zone to expand your impact on the global playground. This gives you freedom. Think about it – what can stop you when you devote your day-to-day to invest in and cultivate your fear-embracing mindset?

To enhance your global influence as a leader, it is crucial to adopt a fear-embracing mindset. This will empower you to skilfully handle the inevitable challenges, rejections and failures that will arise during your journey. How you respond to these obstacles will ultimately determine your success or failure, highlighting the importance of cultivating a well-trained mind.

The mind is conditioned to protect and serve us, leading to fight or flight responses in many situations. The mental workout here is to stop and analyse these reactions and feelings and to find rational ways to change or recondition them to favour the intentions and goals of modern life.

Feel your fears and move forward. The more you face, embrace, act and rethink your fears, the more flexible you'll become in navigating the international waters of human interactions, and life in general.

CASE STORY – 'JOSE, I'M SCARED TO TAKE ACTION!'

Emily was coming back from maternity leave and dove straight into one of my 'Presenting with impact' workshops. She works in the sales department of a big events business and decided to join because she was fearful of delivering presentations to large audiences. She explained that her fear stems from a combination of factors, including a lack of confidence, fear of judgement and past negative experiences.

I checked in with her and she was happy to be an active participant and to engage in all activities, so I invited her to tell a story in front of the group. All attendees did this and they all felt nervous but did well in the end. I delivered more content followed by additional activities where she and the rest of the group needed to stand up and present something.

During these sessions, it's a real privilege to see how participants embrace their fears and act regardless. That takes courage.

Emily kept on pushing herself, feeling scared but doing it anyway. By the end of the day, she was a different person. Her body language had completely shifted and she shared how she felt her confidence had improved.

The results she achieved wouldn't have been even close to what they were had she not taken massive action while feeling scared. It was great to see her shine.

Next time something scares you, think about the growth
that awaits you on the other side of that fear. That's where
success is.

Self-reflection

- How well do you currently prepare for
  challenging situations or potential problems in
  your personal and professional life?

- How would you rate your international
  communication intelligence on a scale from one
  to ten? And what can you do to improve it?

- Are you open to adjusting your communication
  style based on the individual you are interacting
  with? How can you adapt your language, tone
  and approach to ensure clearer understanding
  and effective communication?

- Have you ever embraced fear as a driving force
  for growth and development in your career
  and life?

- What's one thing that you fear and what will you
  do about it after reading this chapter?

Action points

- Fail to prepare, prepare to fail. Make your global influence development a daily habit. You can practise it and improve every day if you wish to.

- IQ and EQ are not as impactful without CQ. Your communication intelligence will allow you to effectively craft messages and communicate in a way that appeals to both rational and emotional realms.

- Start putting together your own global influence toolkit with your favourite frameworks.

- The global influence mantras will help you cultivate your focus, clarity, motivation, encouragement, self-awareness and self-regulation.

- Adopt a fear-embracing mindset and use it to keep on growing and moving forward. Fear is a great ally when you use it well.

EIGHT

Applying Your Global Influence

In chapter two, I presented the core areas of global influence as the mind, heart and body, and explained how depending on where we are acting from (mind, heart or heart–mind) our body would represent this differently. There could also be inaction, which is when we feel and think but don't act. Then, in chapter five I explained the variable levels of energy there can be in human interactions within the international playground. Next, I'm going to provide you with a structure that combines these learnings to support your international communications.

Chillies, avocados and ice creams

I had to come up with some cool names for these behavioural styles and, as you know, I love food (remember the tacos?), so when we combine the different energy levels with the mind, heart and body framework, we end up with: chillies, avocados and ice creams. I bet you didn't see this one coming.

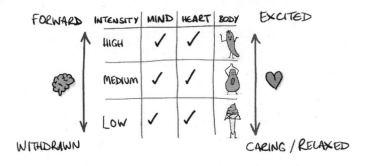

These fluctuating human behaviours are represented in the next illustration. As you can see, their intensity can change from country to country and for an individual, depending on the context of the interaction.

In this section, I'm going to show you how you can positively influence the chillies, avocados and ice creams using the 3Cs from chapter six. But first, I'd like to start by reminding you that the chilli, avocado and ice cream analogy is an oversimplification of the behaviours people show when interacting with others. Therefore, this structure is not a rigid prescription because, in the end, we are all different and complex. So where do you start if you want to positively influence the people you lead?

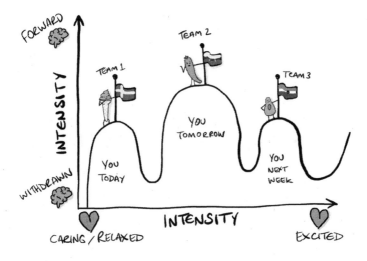

You can start by recognising initial traits, while injecting some healthy humour. That will help reduce fears, tensions and pressures that may exist or emerge and will give you the upper hand in the influencing process. For example, when I come across a chilli style, because of their dominant and upfront behaviour, just saying to myself, 'Oh, I have a chilli in front of me,' helps me to relax, take some of the emotions out and become more objective. It also enables me to think on my feet. Ultimately, what I'm doing is adapting my style to the person and, more specifically, to the behaviour they're exhibiting in that specific situation.

Generally, when I deal with an avocado, I tend to increase my empathy and attractiveness. And when in front of an ice cream I ramp up my compelling energy by utilising more factual information, frameworks and theory to back up my points.

It's important, though, that you don't box people in. The same person currently exhibiting chilli behaviour, in a different environment might show the behaviours of an avocado or an ice cream. The great thing is that you will be able to recognise them and act accordingly.

As you move forward, use the chilli, avocado and ice cream analogy as a frame of reference. Throughout, remain vigilant for any shifts in behaviour and address any fight or flight responses that may arise. Your fear-embracing mindset will be your steady companion, allowing you to navigate and confront challenges with resilience and determination.

Taming the chilli

The chillies are the people who generally bring the heat to their human interactions. They speak up and out, can be seen as direct and, on occasion, aggressive. They are highly driven, egocentric, competitive, bring loads of emotions to their communication and tend to use lively hand gestures and big facial expressions. They speak fast and with a strong tone.

You will find them ready to deliver a presentation, direct people, give advice and instructions. They are great at motivating and inspiring people because of their ability to communicate openly. They are also highly passionate, action-driven individuals who enjoy taking control of situations. I call them 'me' people, because it's all about them. I also call them cheerful people. Their attractiveness is high.

As explained in chapter two, you can break this category of behaviour down further for additional flexibility in your understanding and approach. There will be the chillies that operate predominantly from the mind and the ones that operate from the heart. What you are likely to notice is less emotion and more rationality, or the other way round.

When acting from the mind, they are more direct, structured and determined. On a bad day, you can expect them to be dominating and pushy. When coming from the heart they are in more of a flow, less directive and more expressive. Under stress, you may notice that they get excitable, frantic and hasty. When their energy intensity drops from high to medium, you will begin to notice subtle changes in behaviours. You will find that some of the styles overlap, and that they can change depending on the context and who they interact with.

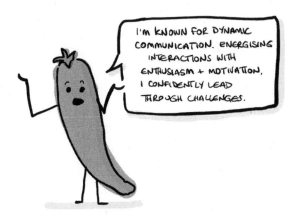

I'M KNOWN FOR DYNAMIC COMMUNICATION. ENERGISING INTERACTIONS WITH ENTHUSIASM + MOTIVATION, I CONFIDENTLY LEAD THROUGH CHALLENGES.

The chilli conveyor

If you are a chilli trying to convey information to another chilli, try not to impose your ideas from the beginning. Regulate your energy and emotions. Be open, look for commonalities instead of differences, especially at the outset. Is the person more rational or open and expressive? Depending on which they are, you can either be concise and direct or engage in more free-flowing conversation.

As an avocado conveying information to a chilli, you may need to increase your energy and emotions to be able to connect with them. Otherwise, they may confuse you with a shy person and either patronise you or fail to respect you or take you seriously. Increase your frankness and be more compelling when providing feedback and when presenting information.

If you're an ice cream, guess what? You need to let some of your own flavour out. It's crucial to reveal more of your emotions and warmth when interacting with chillies. If you come off as too distant, you risk extinguishing their enthusiasm. Ice creams tend to come across as quite compelling, but remember to tailor the amount of information you share. Chilli personalities tend to be big-picture visionaries, so bombarding them with excessive details might be overwhelming.

The chilli coach

For chillies, when diving into coaching, it's crucial that you slow down your speaking and thinking, that you pay attention and listen attentively – or, even better, empathetically. Put yourself in the shoes of the person you are engaging with, whether they're a chilli, avocado or ice cream. As chillies' preferred style tends to be the conveyor, the main stretch will be to dedicate time to developing your questioning techniques, being patient and enjoying the silences. Remember that coaching is more about pulling than pushing information; your aim is to allow the other person to come up with their own answers and strategies.

The chilli challenger

Let's look at how chillies are likely to deal with conflict and difficult conversations. Right away, I can tell you that chillies tend not to back away from speaking their mind, but this can only be productive in certain scenarios – just like accommodating the other person's perspective, which is common for an avocado, or completely avoiding it, which, on occasion, can be the go-to reaction of ice creams. Chillies who tend to speak their mind and stick to their guns may want to try to regulate their emotions in order to become more assertive. Explore different reactions, like collaborating with the other person to find a mutually satisfactory resolution, or even accommodating the other person to give them an opportunity. For

163

example, if you have a team member who sometimes makes decisions you don't agree with, instead of always directing so that things happen as you expect, let the person see their decisions through. There could be a lesson for you both.

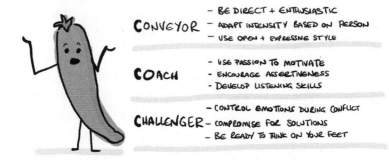

CONVEYOR
- BE DIRECT + ENTHUSIASTIC
- ADAPT INTENSITY BASED ON PERSON
- USE OPEN + EXPRESSIVE STYLE

COACH
- USE PASSION TO MOTIVATE
- ENCOURAGE ASSERTIVENESS
- DEVELOP LISTENING SKILLS

CHALLENGER
- CONTROL EMOTIONS DURING CONFLICT
- COMPROMISE FOR SOLUTIONS
- BE READY TO THINK ON YOUR FEET

For chillies, doing what can at times seem counterintuitive may lead to greater learning.

Earning the avocado's respect

Think for a moment of an avocado, but not just any avocado. A perfect avocado from a tropical country with lots of flavour and a creamy texture. It's very different to a chilli, yet the two together can be delicious. An avocado doesn't need to shout for people to notice them in the room. They have a quiet and calm presence that, overall, conveys respect and closeness. People who have this as their preferred style focus on listening more than speaking, and on empathising rather than fixating on their own feelings. I describe them as 'you' people – their focus is predominantly on others. They are ready to support and can be good coaches because of their strong listening and questioning skills. They are not too cheerful, nor too serious. They are balanced and so is their compelling attractiveness. They won't set the house on fire, unlike the chillies. They use their mind to proactively listen and their heart to know what it feels like to experience the other person's reality. They are friendly, people-oriented and loyal.

Just like chillies, the avocado can act from the mind and also from the heart. When their actions are mind-driven, they are prompted to listen to respond and not necessarily to understand; they focus more on structure and what needs to be done, and can become very organised and task-driven. Under stress, they may struggle with uncertainty, managing their time effectively and building connections. When they act from the heart, their behaviour becomes more about serving and caring for individuals. On a bad day, they can be too supportive, agreeable and docile.

One stretch for avocados can be to proactively pick a side, since they have a tendency to take the middle ground as advocates in conflict situations or debates. My invitation to avocados, as usual, is first to always look for balance between heart and mind, and then develop your ability to move around the different global influence styles.

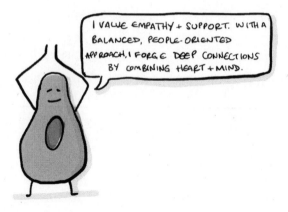

The avocado conveyor

If you are an avocado conveying information to another, especially when providing developmental feedback, make sure you say what you want to say but be cautious in your choice of words. The challenge here generally is to say it in a way that impacts the behaviour you'd like the other person to change.

When a chilli engages with an avocado, my advice is to be more empathetic, slow down and to not make assumptions, especially negative ones, because the avocado communicates at a different pace, in a different tone and can be more withdrawn.

If you're an ice cream, it is important to choose a more personable approach when communicating with an avocado and to focus on feelings as well as facts. Look to provide safety for the other person and show that you care. Be patient and don't overload the conversation with too many details and complicated terminology. Give the other person space to express themselves.

The avocado coach

For an avocado, coaching may be a more natural style. The complexities will be different depending on who you are coaching. For an outgoing chilli, the challenge is to build enough rapport so that they begin to answer your questions and play your game. It's important that you are firm and assertive to maintain connection, but appeal to their emotions.

When coaching an ice cream, explain what you are doing and frame the conversation by letting them know you will be asking a few more questions than usual and, if possible, share with them the reason behind some of the questions you are asking. Remember they are likely to be analysing what you are saying as well as thinking about their answers.

Coaching another avocado? Agree on an expected outcome for the coaching to keep the conversation on track and avoid unnecessary questions. Make sure their answers are honest and not intended simply to please your ears. Avocados tend to be amiable and will look to avoid saying something that they think the other person may not want to hear.

The avocado challenger

For avocados that may be prompted to automatically give away the last slice of pizza or jump into building a puzzle with the other person, try sticking to your guns sometimes if you feel strongly about a decision or point of view. Be prepared to feel uncomfortable and deal with any fears or rejection, not being liked or upsetting the individual you are communicating with. The beauty of debating points of view is that it enables you to better understand each other, even if you don't immediately find a resolution.

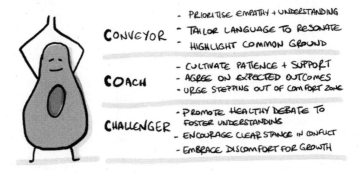

CONVEYOR
- PRIORITISE EMPATHY + UNDERSTANDING
- TAILOR LANGUAGE TO RESONATE
- HIGHLIGHT COMMON GROUND

COACH
- CULTIVATE PATIENCE + SUPPORT
- AGREE ON EXPECTED OUTCOMES
- URGE STEPPING OUT OF COMFORT ZONE

CHALLENGER
- PROMOTE HEALTHY DEBATE TO FOSTER UNDERSTANDING
- ENCOURAGE CLEAR STANCE IN CONFLICT
- EMBRACE DISCOMFORT FOR GROWTH

 Getting out of their balanced zone will increase avocados' compelling attractiveness.

Enticing the ice cream

Ice creams, as their name implies, have a distinct flavour, but they will sit behind the counter waiting for you to appeal to them. The glass is the separation that needs to be bridged. Within this framework, they are the most analytical people in terms of communication and are particularly good at not showing their feelings, especially in the early stages.

I describe them as 'the thing' people, for their ability to separate tasks from feelings. Can you understand now why they can be the opposite to chillies? They are detailed, professional, factual and to the point. I call them serious people. They are more compelling than attractive.

Since some of their traits are to be more rational and less emotional, they can bring great insights to their conversations, because they are deep thinkers. This is when they give me brain freeze. I ask myself, 'Where did that moment of brilliance come from?' If only they spoke more often, without overthinking things sometimes.

When they act from the mind, they can be direct with a level of bluntness. This can also mean they are perceived as arrogant or aggressive, but different from the chillies because their intensity tends to be lower. These people are more composed. On a bad day, they may be indecisive, get colder and more reserved.

When they act from the heart (definitely not their strongest suit), they can struggle sharing their feelings and may end up not expressing how they truly feel. Under pressure, they may refrain from acting altogether.

The ice cream conveyor

Ice creams want details; if you are one ice cream dealing with another, be careful with information overload and inaction. When providing feedback, for example, share one thing at a time and make sure it is understood by the other person. Be flexible with your expectations and remember that your way is not always the right way.

Chillies, be patient and know that it may take more time for an ice cream to warm up to you, so don't get too pushy; provide more details and back up your points with additional facts if need be.

Ice creams and avocados – who will speak first? For the avocado, don't expect too many feelings to come your way and look to adapt your language, moving from feelings towards facts.

The ice cream coach

The ice cream, as a coach, can be highly knowledge-able but have a tendency to overthink things. If this is you, you should try to ask more spontaneous and curious questions aimed at helping the other person shift their views or behaviours to ones that will be more helpful for them and the business.

Overthinking may lead to assumptions that are not necessarily true, so again, asking questions will help you uncover the reality for the other person. Get out of your own head, listen empathetically and be patient with the emotions that could potentially be coming your way every time you ask a question – unless you're coaching another ice cream. In this case, make sure questions and answers are not being overcompli-cated to ensure there is a clear outcome at the end of the conversation.

The ice cream challenger

Ice creams may need to process things at their own pace to be as certain as possible about what they are going to say; hence, delaying conflict may be a recurring issue for them. If you're an ice cream, my suggestion is that you try thinking on your feet and having a conversation on the spot, because that unique opportunity to make an impact may not come again. Explore your flexibility and look to collaborate more often, since your preference may be to operate alone. As an ice cream, a great question to ask yourself in a conflict situation is: 'What reaction would be the most beneficial?'

Go out and try to learn from real-life experiences. If needed, you can always apologise and explain what the intentions behind your reaction were. This would mean you are being intentional, and that there is reasoning behind your actions.

Listening, curiosity and caring for the other person will help you to connect and find ways in which you can influence them. Take cultural differences and any language gap into consideration. This applies to all human engagements, whether conveying, coaching or challenging – for chillies, avocados or ice creams.

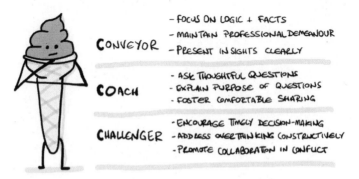

CONVEYOR
- FOCUS ON LOGIC + FACTS
- MAINTAIN PROFESSIONAL DEMEANOUR
- PRESENT INSIGHTS CLEARLY

COACH
- ASK THOUGHTFUL QUESTIONS
- EXPLAIN PURPOSE OF QUESTIONS
- FOSTER COMFORTABLE SHARING

CHALLENGER
- ENCOURAGE TIMELY DECISION-MAKING
- ADDRESS OVERTHINKING CONSTRUCTIVELY
- PROMOTE COLLABORATION IN CONFLICT

Given the complexity involved in covering all scenarios and the subjective nature of communication due to diverse realities, personalities and behaviours, it's crucial not to assume but to observe keenly and adjust your approach. Use these analogies to recognise and positively influence temporary behaviours in those you lead.

CASE STORY – 'JOSE, THEY DON'T SEEM TO UNDERSTAND WHAT I MEAN!'

A client once said to me: 'Jose, the problem I'm having is that when I delegate, the team seem to understand, don't tend to say much in terms of feedback and then get the task wrong and I end up doing it myself.'

Olivia was based in America, managing her team over in Malaysia. Over an online coaching call, she presented her problem with such vibrancy and energy that I had to explain the international behavioural styles analogy to her because she was coming across as a high-intensity, forward-mind chilli, but also with a level of excited heart. In my mind I thought, 'Would I tell her I didn't understand if she delegated a task to me? Hell no!'

I shared this with her, and she laughed. 'You have a point, Jose,' she agreed.

Next, I moved on to explore with her the behavioural styles of her Malaysian team. Looking at the traits of each style, Olivia agreed that many of them were showing avocado and ice cream behaviours, and she understood how her style of communicating might have been quite intense for them.

> The last time I had a catch-up with Olivia, she said that communication had massively improved and that her team had been opening up more to her. Their performance was better, and she was feeling more relaxed when speaking with them.

 Be aware of your own behavioural style in order to flex it when communicating with your teams and people within the organisation. The same applies when speaking to clients, suppliers and other stakeholders.

Self-reflection

- Who shows the intensity of energy and behaviours typical of a chilli, an avocado or an ice cream within your work environment?

- Are you effectively adapting to various behavioural styles in international interactions?

- Do you categorise people too narrowly, and how can you change this?

- How do you handle conflict across diverse behavioural styles?

- What steps can you take to enhance coaching skills for different preferences?

Action points

- Recognise whether someone's behaviour aligns more with a dominant, expressive 'chilli', an empathetic, listener 'avocado', or an analytical, composed 'ice cream'.

- Tailor your communication strategies so that you can effectively convey information, coach and navigate conflict whether interacting with a chilli, avocado or ice cream behavioural style.

- Get curious about the interactions between the different styles and look at what works and what doesn't work when you exercise your global influence. Learning from failure and feedback will be part of the process. Use the analogy as guidance – there are no absolutes when it comes to human interactions. And always remain malleable.

- Implement what you've learned and enjoy the ride.

NINE

Amplifying Your Global Influence

To amplify your influence, it's important that you prepare and continuously apply what you learn throughout your leadership career and life. The process never stops and doesn't happen overnight; thus, flexibility, ownership and consistency will be paramount. As you continue to positively influence others, they will do the same, and so will the people they impact, because of your ability and desire to create impact and change. This is the compound effect of your global influence, and this is how you will amplify your reach.

This book is a way for me to amplify my message and influence, which, as you already know, comes from the impact that incredible humans have had on me. This is what I want for you: to be one of them, the authentic humans leading people to always become greater versions of themselves.

Influencing an audience

I couldn't finish this book without sharing my knowledge and insights on how to present with impact and confidence to amplify your influence and elevate your people as well as any audience. Presenting would fall under conveying, one of the 3Cs, because you are essentially communicating with an audience, although it's not a one-way stream as some people think. Influencing an audience is about creating a dialogue with them, along with a deep connection that can lead to a shift in mindset, behaviours and/or a call to action.

 When you present, you don't speak at people – you speak with them.

Have you ever been to a presentation after which you either wanted to speak to the presenter or couldn't wait to implement some of the content shared? This means you were in the presence of an influential speaker, which is what I intend for you to become. For some people, it comes naturally; for others, it can be trickier. Regardless, it is essential that, as a leader, you work on developing these skills so that you are capable of standing up and sharing your message with impact. Try and think of some influential leaders who aren't great public speakers – you may struggle here, because they all understand how important this is for any leadership career.

I remember when, at twelve years old, my teacher, Marcos Subero, told me I had to learn how to speak in public if I wanted to be successful in life. He also told me to read the newspapers. Hey, at least I took the first tip seriously. Gerald Rudolph Ford, ex-President of the United States, once said (I'm paraphrasing here) that if he went back to school, he would focus on speaking in front of an audience because there is nothing more important than the ability to communicate effectively. I hope I've given you enough ammunition to read further. This is a topic that could be covered in a separate book, but I'm going to squeeze my brain to give you what I consider some of the most important elements for you to work on.

It's all about certainty. Within a business context, when you present you are transferring certainty about yourself as the speaker and expert, about the project, product or service and about the business you represent. Depending on how you present, you will be either increasing or decreasing the audience's certainty levels.

Focus on the following and you are onto a winning presentation – it will help you to be your BEST every time you walk on stage:

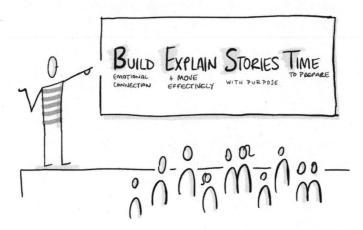

Build an emotional connection

You need to do this right from the start. You may have heard before that a first impression is built in the first few seconds of people seeing you; hence, it's vital that you feel confident and comfortable with yourself and the content you are going to deliver. This is the strategy I recommend:

- Connect with your **passion** for the topic you're going to deliver. Ask yourself, 'What do I like and enjoy so much about this subject? What positive impact will it have on the audience?'

- Do a lot of preparation to make sure you bring your **A game**. Work on both your self-confidence and your competence. What gives you confidence in this scenario? What don't you know yet? What does your audience know? Make sure to cover all the angles and to know your content inside out.

- **Believe in yourself**, the topic and your preparation. Your presentation will be special because there is nothing vanilla about you. You will bring a unique spin because the message is coming from you – based on your knowledge and experience. This last part is about self-assurance and reflection.

The next thing to think about is how to hook them with a bold statement, question, quote, statistic or an impactful image. When I speak about confidence in presenting, I sometimes start with this question: 'Have you ever been paralysed and unable to speak?' Many people in the audience will connect with this, which is more powerful than saying, 'Hello everyone,' don't you think?

Explain and move effectively

The explaining part is about having a structure that revolves around your core message or topic. This is what will enable you to share the information you want to convey while making sure you bring the audience along with you. A great way to start is by thinking about what you would like your listeners to take away or do after you have delivered your session.

Once you are clear on this, you can work on the body of your presentation. Here is a simple yet impactful structure that I use:

1. Hook

2. Introduction

3. First message

4. Second message

5. Third message

6. Conclusion and call to action

As I'm going through my messages, I make sure that I follow the 3Ts:

1. Tell them what you are going to tell them.

2. Tell them that thing.

3. Tell them what you just told them.

You may have noticed this structure throughout the book, which is intended to create a seamless flow for the reader. You want to create the same experience for your listeners when you present.

Now onto the 'move' part. This is about stage positioning. The term comes from the theatrical arts, where the stage is divided into nine sections or positions. Next time you go to a play, pay attention to how the performers use the stage for greater impact.

For the purpose of speaking, you can move anywhere you like and anchor different areas of the stage, but as a starting point and a rule of thumb I recommend dividing it into three areas. This will also give you more flexibility, since stages tend to be different sizes. Also, if you are behind a lectern (which I don't like because it can be restrictive in terms of mobility), you will still be able to use your torso and body language to guide the audience through the three areas.

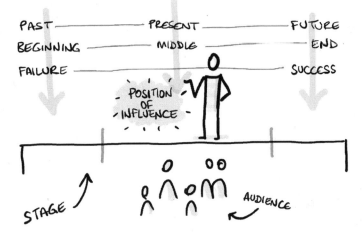

In order to be intentional and consistent with your actions and movements on stage, I recommend anchoring the beginning of your story, the problem, pains, failures to your right (left for the audience). The middle, which is your position of influence, is where you should start and finish your talk; it can also be used for the middle of the story, a transition or the present. Then move towards your left (the audience's right) for the solution, happiness, success and ending.

If, like I mentioned, you're behind a lectern, you will still be able to indicate these areas with your torso and hand gestures, which will increase the impact of your words.

Using stage positioning will add depth to the stories you tell, which, as you are about to find out, you can also create using a three-step structure.

 Rely on the power of three when crafting and delivering impactful presentations.

Stories with purpose

Stories will make you and your presentation stand out, as long as you tell them well and with purpose. Make sure they are original, illustrate your point and are concise. This links back to explaining effectively. Stories will also help you create the emotional bond with your audience, so it's important that you spend time developing your storytelling skills.

The IPS structure works well in business storytelling. It is as follows:

- **I** – Introduction or premise (beginning)

- **P** – Problem or situation (middle)

- **S** – Solution and results (end)

Here is a story that I crafted using the IPS structure:

I: After two years of trying to get my foot through the door, I finally managed to close an appointment with the person responsible for the product I was promoting. I was only allowed a fifteen-minute face-to-face visit, during which I had to understand their main pains and challenges to be able to come up with an initial angle that would get them interested in having a second meeting.

P: Time and capacity were significant issues for them, so I offered the option to recreate one of their features at our place in the UK and to come back to present the savings through a new manufacturing strategy. A couple of years later, we had managed to save this business over one million euros in time and capacity. It took me two years to open the door, and only fifteen minutes to keep them interested and engaged. This was a top-ten worldwide aerospace manufacturer.

S: It's important to always be ready, to think on your feet and to use all your knowledge and skills to positively influence people. Fifteen minutes can change your business, and can also change your life.

The above is a real story from my selling days, and is one of many short stories that I use in my presentations to illustrate my points.

Since lack of storytelling is one of the challenges I come across when coaching C-level executives and business leaders on how to become more influential speakers, I always like to share my aerospace client story, and I tell it using stage positioning areas for stronger results. Not only can stories be used to connect with and inspire an audience, but they are also powerful selling tools.

I recommend that you start building up your repertoire of stories and, next time you have a presentation, hopefully you will already have a good story you can use. The more you think about stories, the more of them you will find. We are natural storytellers; our life itself is a story created by our mind.

Time to prepare

Never go and wing it, the impact won't be the same and, even if people tell you how great you did, you will know it could have been better. Take time to bring all the above together, create your presentation, design your slides (if you are planning to use them) to support your presentation, craft your stories, use your body and tonality and practise, practise, practise. You can record yourself and send it to people you trust, asking for their constructive feedback. To ensure the information you receive helps you improve, share with them the feedback structure from chapter six.

As a rule of thumb, prepare until you feel nervous but fully capable of rocking the stage. Nerves will always be present but it's important that you learn to manage them. If you feel that your butterflies are out of control, instruct them to fly in formation. And if, after all of this, you still don't rock the stage, learn from your failure quickly and get ready for your next presentation. Do your best every time, deliver a heart–mind–body experience to your listeners and continue to grow and expand as an influential leader.

Impacting your people and your business growth

After reading this book, a new you should emerge to create positive change within your organisation, starting with your people and how you lead them to lead themselves. I invite you to share your main takeaways from this book with your team and explain how you plan to roll them out so that you are all on the same page. Whenever you or any team member acquires new knowledge, it's essential to present it to everyone else, as it will impact your culture and communication. If, for example, after finishing the book you decide to proactively implement feedback, coaching and healthy conflict, introduce your people to what you've learned, explain to them why you believe it's important and open up the floor for discussion as to how it can all be implemented.

Getting your people onboard is the first step. This is like asking for permission and getting their approval to start communicating differently amongst each other; to ask more questions; to be more open and direct with feedback; to be more honest and vulnerable; to use humour instead of unhealthy banter; to develop multicultural awareness and flexibility when interacting with each other and external stakeholders like clients, partners and suppliers.

This is how you begin to impact the bottom line of your organisation; you start by building trust through improved communication, which then leads to greater mutual understanding, better relationships, increased cultural sensitivity and international awareness and, ultimately, a stronger commitment towards the organisation's goals and objectives. Your global influence leadership will not only trickle down through the business, but it will also have an impact upwards, sideways and in all possible directions. It will get you noticed because of the results your teams will achieve and the levels of motivation your employees will show; it will also be reflected in the feedback you receive from them.

The frameworks, concepts and insights contained in this book can, for example, be applied to effective delegation, to ensure that you are giving people the opportunity to take on new tasks and challenges to develop them further. This will also help you to understand what their strengths, limitations and needs are through your improved abilities to convey information, coach effectively and challenge unhelpful behaviours. In terms of performance management, think about how your increased influence levels will impact your daily communications with your team members, including one-to-ones and appraisals.

As you have experienced, a big part of this book has to do with mindset, how we think and interact with our global environment and the people within it; how we manage and benefit from fear; how to be more authentic and less vanilla. As a result of these mindset shifts, you and the people you lead can become more resilient in the face of adversity, which will have a knock-on effect on everyone's mental health, relationships, performance and overall wellbeing.

Next time you need to speak in front of an audience, you now have a structure you can use to craft your presentation as well as highly engaging business-relevant stories that will position you as an authority in the minds of your audience. The structure can be applied to your daily meetings, sales and marketing presentations, year-end presentations and more. If you wish to start speaking outside your businesses, the world is your oyster.

Your enhanced global influence will help you to attract new talent to your business. Ultimately, who doesn't want to be led by a caring, resourceful, authentic and impactful individual? In fact, there will be many who don't – that's OK because the ones who do will be clear as to why they recognise you as their leader. Through your new global influence lens, you will be able to choose your tribe and your tribe will choose you.

In this ever-changing global economy, adaptive and authentic leadership is fundamental to creating and growing businesses that can withstand market forces while providing value to society and the workforce. One way to achieve this is by continuously empowering multicultural groups of people to cultivate intrinsic motivation, authenticity, vulnerability and honesty. By encouraging them to act with purpose and communicate effectively, fostering a collaborative and harmonious work environment and supporting and holding each other accountable. These are essential steps to reaching greater organisational objectives and personal growth.

CASE STORY – 'JOSE, I'M SORRY BUT READING OFF A SCRIPT DOESN'T WORK FOR ME!'

This is what Sven, the COO of SEAT-CUPRA said to me during a coaching session, as he was preparing to speak at a big event in Germany where the company would be launching one of their electric SUVs.

It was music to my ears because I don't like to present using scripts either. In fact, I coach people to speak without them. Instead of relying on scripts, I teach a structure, which enables speakers to be engaging, deliberate and, above all, free to express themselves while keeping their message on point.

Sven was animated and liked telling stories. Together, we worked on putting some structure around it so that he could present CUPRA's exponential experience to large crowds over several days.

We built his story using a simple beginning, middle and end structure and, for additional impact, I showed Sven how to use stage anchors so that he could move purposefully as he was unveiling his story.

I was lucky enough to be there for his first presentation, which was a success, just like the rest of the show.

Use structure, tell relevant stories to illustrate your points and move with purpose on stage.

Self-reflection

- How can you develop a deep sense of connection with your audience when presenting, and how does this impact your ability to influence and create change?

- What strategies can you implement to structure your presentations effectively, ensuring a clear message and impactful delivery that resonates with your audience?

- How can you harness the power of storytelling to enhance your presentations, create emotional connections and leave a lasting impact on your audience?

- How do you currently approach preparation for presentations and public speaking engagements, and how can you improve your skills to confidently engage and inspire your listeners?

- In what ways can you leverage your enhanced global influence to create a positive shift in your organisation's culture, communication dynamics and overall business performance?

Action points

- Strengthen your presenting skills through dedicated practice and meticulous preparation. Avoid improvisation; comprehensive groundwork is essential for success.

- Seek speaking opportunities both within your organisation and externally, as they can significantly enhance your recognition and visibility within your company.

- Rely on the power of three when structuring your presentation, crafting your stories and moving purposefully on stage.

- Apply the BEST model to become a more influential speaker.

- Introduce and integrate feedback, coaching and conflict-resolution practices for improved communication and trust within your organisation.

- Encourage team members to develop inner motivation, be authentic and communicate openly by applying the concepts and frameworks from this book.

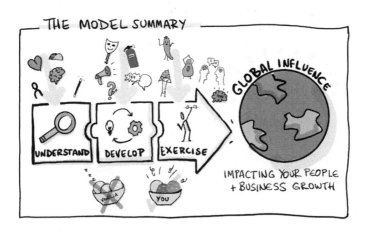

Conclusion

Alright, it's time to put a bow on this. I hope you had a great time going through some of my stories and, most importantly, that you are coming away with some clear thoughts and actions with regards to how you can simplify, improve and amplify your ability to lead and influence others across nations.

Exercising your global influence can be SIMPLER than you think; follow the frameworks with flexibility and always adapt to the person you are communicating with. Check in with yourself often and gauge where you are communicating from, whether heart or mind (or both), and make sure you act when it benefits the interaction between the parties. Follow the global influence magic formula and let it unravel:

> Global Influence = Hard and Consistent Work +
> Passion + Vision + People

Whenever you feel fear of failure or rejection, or a need to fit in, think about the ice cream parlour, how by launching the avocado flavour they grew exponentially and won a Guinness World Record. Always look to be less vanilla and more you. This will help you attract the right people, circumstances and results into your career and life. It will also have a more authentic impact on the people you lead and interact with. You and your leadership will be memorable.

Enjoy playing and experimenting with the energy intensity in human interactions and observing the international behavioural styles analogy in action. By identifying these styles in your human interactions, you will be more self-aware and prepared to effectively apply the 3Cs. In all cases, remain an explorer, learner and stretcher.

Inject excitement, admiration, humour and humility to your human interactions, just like my grandad did. Grab a TACO with your team and clients, develop your POWER and focus your attention on the process and the progress you make daily. Develop your own range of global influence tools and frameworks and begin to notice positive change in you, your people and your business results.

As you begin to exercise your global influence, introduce your team to some of the concepts and frameworks so that they understand where you are operating from and what's driving the change in how you communicate and engage with them. The content of this book doesn't only apply to leadership, it will also impact relationships with clients, suppliers and stakeholders.

Remember that what makes the content of this book impactful is not just the amount of people you touch as a result of applying what you've learned, but the compound effect derived from the people they in turn will impact because of your influence. Focus on one person at a time and see the magic unfold globally.

A final gift: scan the below QR code to access my World-Class Communicator online course, completely free.

Love, respect and much success,
Jose

References

Chapter 1: It's All About Impact

Banerjee, A, 'Cultural intelligence a new imperative', *Business Standard* (4 January 2015), www.business-standard.com/article/management/cultural-intelligence-a-new-imperative-115010400584_1.html, accessed December 2022

Carpenter, G and Wyman, O, *M&A Beyond Borders: Opportunities and risks* (MMC, 2008), https://graphics.eiu.com/upload/eb/marsh_cross_border_report.pdf, accessed August 2023

Dilts, R, 'Robert Dilts explains NLP logical levels of learning & change + impact of trauma (Part 1)' (2018), www.youtube.com/watch?v=hrK9_ZPo790&t=28s, accessed August 2022

Gino, F, 'The business case for curiosity', *Harvard Business Review* (September–October, 2018), https://hbr.org/2018/09/the-business-case-for-curiosity, accessed August 2023

Hewitt, A, *Culture integration in M&A: Survey findings* (Aon, 2011), www.aon.com/attachments/thought-leadership/M_A_Survey.pdf, accessed August 2023

Thought Farmer, 'Culture clash is the reason mergers fail' (Thought Farmer, 9 October 2014), www.thoughtfarmer.com/blog/culture-clash-mergers-software, accessed October 2022

Chapter 3: The Magnetic Effect Of Global Influence

Carnegie, D, *How to win Friends and Influence People in the Digital Age* (Simon & Schuster, 2011)

Lencioni, P, *The Five Dysfunctions of a Team: A leadership fable* (John Wiley & Sons, 2002)

Chapter 4: Authenticity

Google Trends, 'Most popular ice-cream flavours worldwide' (Google Trends, 27 March 2023), https://trends.google.com/trends/explore?date=today%205-y&q=vanilla%20ice%20cream,%2Fm%2F0h1bv8c,strawberry%20ice%20cream,coconut%20ice%20cream&hl=en-GB, accessed March 2023

Pink, D, *Drive: The surprising truth about what motivates us* (Riverhead Hardcover, 2009)

Wikipedia, 'Heladeria Coromoto' (Wikipedia, 24 June 2013), https://en.wikipedia.org/wiki/Helader%C3%ADa_Coromoto, accessed January 2022

Chapter 5: Internationality

Is Accurate, 'Cultures around the world' (Is Accurate, 26 March 2021), https://isaccurate.com/blog/cultures-around-the-world, accessed 20 April 2023

Lingua, 'How many languages are there in the world?' (Lingua, 29 June 2022), https://lingua.edu/how-many-languages-are-there-in-the-world, accessed April 2023

National Geographic, 'Continent', *National Geographic* (27 July 2022), https://education.nationalgeographic.org/resource/Continent, accessed April 2023

Ong, S, *Energize: Make the most of every moment* (Penguin Random House UK, 2022)

Oxford Languages Dictionary, 'Excitement' (Google, no date), www.google.com/search?q=excitement+definition&rlz=1C1CHBF_en-GBGB812GB812&oq=excitement+de&aqs=chrome.1.69i57j0i512l9.4348j1j7&sourceid=chrome&ie=UTF-8, accessed May 2023

United Nations, 'About us' (UN, no date), www.un.org/en/about-us, accessed April 2023

Chapter 6: The Channels Of Global Influence

Benson, K, 'The magic relationship ratio, according to science' (The Gottman Institute, no date), www.gottman. com/blog/the-magic-relationship-ratio-according-science, accessed May 2023

Kilmann, R, 'The eight key attributes of a conflict situation: When to use each conflict-handling mode most effectively' (Kilmann Diagnostics, no date), https://kilmanndiagnostics.com/the-eight-key-attributes-of-a-conflict-situation, accessed May 2023

University of Oxford, 'Styles of influencing', *People and Organisational Development* (no date), www.mpls.ox.ac. uk/files/training/styles-of-influencing, accessed January 2023

Chapter 7: Fail To Prepare, Prepare To Fail

Holiday, R and Hanselman, S, *The Daily Stoic: 366 meditations on wisdom, perseverance, and the art of living* (Profile Books, 2016)

tcgagency, 'About CQ: Clare Munn at Ted Women' (YouTube, 17 March 2011), www.youtube.com/ watch?v=ig44XT6Tw1w&ab_channel=tcgagency, accessed October 2023

Chapter 9: Amplifying Your Global Influence

Anderson, C, *TEDTalks: The official TED guide to public speaking* (NB Publishing, 2018)

BBC Bitesize, 'Stage positioning', (BBC Bitesize, no date), www.bbc.co.uk/bitesize/guides/zm2yt39/revision/2, accessed January 2023

Bersin, J, 'Building the Simply Irresistible Organization – Josh Bersin' (2015), www.youtube.com/watch?v=eJLbJnRk6ng, accessed July 2022

Further Reading

Amabile, TM and Kramer, SJ, 'The power of small wins', *Harvard Business Review* (May 2011), https://hbr.org/2011/05/the-power-of-small-wins

Belfort, J, *Way of the Wolf: Straight line selling: Master the art of persuasion, influence, and success* (John Murray Learning, 2017)

Blanchard, K and Conley, R, *Simple Truths of Leadership* (Berrett-Koehler, 2022)

Bowden, M, *Winning Body Language: Control the conversation, command attention, and convey the right message – without saying a word* (McGraw-Hill, 2010)

Chapman, G, *The 5 Love Languages: The secret to love that lasts* (Moody Press, 2015)

Cialdini, R, *Influence: The psychology of persuasion* (Harper Collins, 2007)

Erikson, T, *Surrounded by Idiots: The four types of human behavior and how to effectively communicate with each in business (and in life)* (St. Martin's Essentials, 2014)

Farrelly, F and Brandsma, J, *Provocative Therapy* (Meta Publications, 1974)

Gallo, C, *Five Stars: The communication secrets to get from good to great* (Macmillan, 2018)

Gallo, C, *Talk Like TED: The 9 public speaking secrets of the world's top minds* (Pan Books, 2017)

Godin, S, *Purple Cow: Transform your business by being remarkable* (Penguin, 2005)

Gray, J, *Men are from Mars, Women are from Venus: The classic guide to understanding the opposite sex* (Harper Thorsons, 2018)

Grinder, M, *Charisma: The art of relationships: Understanding the 'cats' and 'dogs' in our lives – an analogy* (Michael Grinder & Associates, 2006)

Kim, C and Mauborgne, R, *Blue Ocean Strategy: How to create uncontested market space and make the competition irrelevant* (Harvard Business School, 2015)

Knight, S, *NLP at Work: Neuro linguistic programming: the essence of excellence*, third edition (NB Publishing, 2009)

Maxwell, J, *The 21 Irrefutable Laws of Leadership: Follow them and people will follow you* (Thomas Nelson, 2007)

McKenna, P, *Instant Confidence: The power to go for anything you want!* (Bantam Press, 2006)

Miller, D, *Building a Story Brand: Clarify your message so customers will listen* (Harper Collins Leadership, 2017)

Oigara, J, *Handbook of Research on Promoting Global Citizenship Education* (IGI Global, 2022)

Page, O, 'How to leave your comfort zone and enter your "growth zone"', PositivePsychology.com (4 November 2020), https://positivepsychology. com/comfort-zone/?utm_content=cmp-true

Peters, S, *The Chimp Paradox: The mind management programme for confidence, success and happiness* (Vermilion, 2012)

Ruiz, M, *The Four Agreements: A practical guide to personal freedom* (Amber-Allen Publishing, 2018)

Sinek, S, *Start With Why: How great leaders inspire everyone to take action* (Portfolio, 2009)

Sinek, S, 'The infinite game: how to lead in the 21st century' (2019), www.youtube.com/ watch?v=3vX2iVIJMFQ

Storoni, M, *Stress-proof: The scientific solution to protect your brain and body – and be more resilient every day* (TarcherPerigee, 2017)

Sullivan, D and Hardy, B, *The Gap and the Gain: The high achievers' guide to happiness, confidence, and success* (Hay House, 2012)

Acknowledgements

I want to thank my grandparents for their uncon-ditional support and guidance. Their lessons and strong values still guide me today. Thank you also to my parents, for bringing me to this world and for being my biggest fans. I love you, *mamá y papá*.

Thanks to my Venezuelan family living in Austra-lia: Tío Juancho, Madrina Julieta, my lovely cousins, Veronica and Sofia, and their beautiful children. You've always taken care of me, especially when I needed you most.

Thank you to my family in Venezuela, especially my cousin Andres, for showing a whole new level of resil-ience and drive to achieve goals in life. Thanks go also to his parents, German and Ana (uncle and aunty), for their incredible energy. You are fun and loving souls.

I want to thank my wife, Ana Bolena, for her love, patience and consistency in her actions to achieve new heights herself while keeping me in check and making sure I achieved my goals too.

Thanks must go also to my brother, German, for his care, love and compassion. He is also in charge of all my videos and livestreams. Thank you so much, brother, for helping me to get my message out there.

My Swedish host families, Asp and Hållams, took care of me and made me feel like one of their own during my exchange student programme. Over twenty-five years have passed and we are still in touch. I look forward to meeting you face-to-face again soon.

A big part of my consistency and determination I owe to my Kajukenbo (a martial arts style) professor, Augusto Troconis. He also showed me the power you find when you do what you love and you inject all of your passion into it. Hand salute, my professor.

Thank you to Conchi Araguren, my first Spanish (or should I say Basque) leader, who gave me the chance to travel to Turkey, Brazil, Argentina, India and so many other countries. She believed in me as an intern and then employed me full-time.

Ramon Cenarruzabeitia, who unfortunately is no longer with us, showed me how to be an international business gentleman. Then, in the UK, Alan Pearce, who you will know by now, taught me so much about business, sales and marketing. David Cawkwell, also not with us anymore, showed me how to be fierce and more daring.

Thank you to Sue Knight, who helped uncover my curiosity and showed me how to be respectfully amused by people's behaviours; to Mike Hopkins, who taught me how to be a better trainer through his direct and challenging style; and to Maria Fran zoni, for her amazing coaching and mentoring that reignited my spark and encouraged me to speak on international communication and influence.

Thank you Toby and Kate McCartney for showing me a unique style of training, teaching me so much and opening my mind to new opportunities. When Toby mentioned that he had done a TEDx, that was my cue. It's so important to surround yourself with amazing people – these are two such people.

Elliot Kay, the master of disaster and my Clubhouse partner in crime, provided me with strong skills and the foundations I needed to become the speaker I am today. He is also a very good friend.

Ernesto Moreno is an amazing soul. This guy was the light in one of my dark hours. I've had some difficult times throughout my life, as we all do. He helped me to redirect my training business while offering his advice, experiences and knowledge without expecting anything in return.

Neil Cameron is an incredible entrepreneur who I found somewhat cocky when we first met at a networking event. He started as a client and is now one of my best friends, always coaching me and making me laugh every time we get together. He has also been incredibly supportive through the book-writing process. Thank you, Nelio.

What about Reza Ram? He is my brother from another mother. He has been there for me since we first met over ten years ago. He was my first client when I began coaching because he wanted to help, and he continues to do so. He was one of my beta readers, helping me to make this book a great one. Thank you, *Recita*!

Cristina Perez Tijeras once said to me, 'Next year will be your year. I believe in you, Jose.' Since then, my business has gone from strength to strength. Thank you, Cristina, for always believing in me. I believe in you too, *hermanita*.

Thank you to Ben and Arnaud, the founders of the WeCoffee community (now called Othership), and all the people I met during countless networking sessions in London. Speaking at many of these events helped me get my message out there while understanding first-hand some of the challenges entrepreneurs were facing in presenting and pitching their ideas with impact and confidence.

I want to thank my amazing beta readers and friends, Nicola Towse at Procter & Gamble, Cecilia Taieb at SEAT-CUPRA, Brigid Farrell at AllTalk Training, and Aitor Zapirain at BSH Group. They dedicated their time to going through the manuscript in order to enrich the content, making it even more relevant, impactful and practical. A special thanks to each one of you for your dedication and for believing in me.

Thanks also to Noel Warnell for the fantastic illustrations he created to make the book a more enjoyable read. They have really brought the text to life.

Thank you to Peter Burbidge from Dale Carnegie London, a good friend and a very picky reader who, along with podcaster and influencer Alex Chisnall, branding and PR strategist Sabrina Stocker, psychotherapist Dr Sabas Castillo, Ricardo Schmidt General Manager at L'Oréal Asia-Pacific, and venture capitalist Leo Castellanos, have inspired and supported my entrepreneurial journey and also provided valuable feedback that has elevated the content of the book.

Thank you to the Venezuelan community worldwide and particularly to Cinzia De Santis, chair and founder of the charity Healing Venezuela, and her team for supporting my efforts and inviting me to speak at their events.

Thank you to Marco Suarez, Miguel Calderon and Gabriela Vasquez for always bringing me joy through their unconditional friendships. You guys are magic.

I could write many more pages of thanks, because so many people have impacted my journey to get me to where I am today. Thank you, everyone. This book is the result of the positive impact you've all had on my life.

The Author

 Jose is an international communication and influence expert. He helps business leaders to build strong and successful international relationships with customers, work colleagues and teams by understanding what it takes to communicate internationally with impact and confidence.

In today's interconnected global landscape, businesses operating across borders, navigating diverse teams and expanding into new markets require clear and impactful cross-cultural communication to foster collaboration, deal with misunderstandings effectively and gain a competitive edge while promoting personal growth.

Jose's writing has been featured on Yahoo Finance and Yahoo News. Some of his articles have been featured on Mentors, Thrive Global, Disrupt Magazine, LA Weekly and The Influencer Age.

Jose is a TEDx speaker and host, professional speaker, leadership and communication trainer, speaking coach, international business and marketing specialist, author of *Global Influence* and founder of Jose Ucar Ltd. He has consistently offered unwavering support to a variety of businesses, including well-known names such as Procter & Gamble, SEAT-CUPRA, DAF Trucks, Amazon, The ExCel London and Chiesi Pharmaceuticals. The outcomes achieved by some of these businesses encompass delivering compelling and impactful presentations at large events, instilling a sense of empowerment in leaders to adeptly navigate challenges, maintain a positive outlook and remain motivated in the face of adversity. Through his encouragement, individuals within these organisations have been prompted to venture beyond their comfort zones, embracing fresh perspectives. As a result, these leaders have fostered personal development among their teams, helping them transform into well-rounded and proficient professionals.

As Jose likes to put it, he is a legal Venezuelan alien living in the UK, who embarked on his international speaking and communication journey at the age of sixteen. For over a decade, Jose was deeply engaged in fostering international relationships among organisations and businesses globally, accomplished through outgoing and incoming commercial missions in partnership with governmental institutions. He also played an instrumental role in sales and marketing, aiding businesses in penetrating and expanding into new markets, while effectively leading international teams.

Over the past six years, Jose has been working with businesses to transform the way they communicate internally and externally, leading to stronger and more authentic relationships with colleagues, employees, and customers. Some of his favourite speaking topics are how to communicate internationally; how to become a more authentic global leader and cultivate a distinctive leadership brand; and how to influence an audience through impactful speaking.

If you'd like to book Jose to speak at your next event or conference, you can connect with him in various ways:

⊕ www.joseucar.com

▣ www.linkedin.com/in/jose-luis-ucar

◎ www.instagram.com/jose_ucar_